Good Night Stories for Rebel Girls

THIS BOOK
BELONGS TO

Ella B-P

Good Night Stories for Rebel Girls

100 Tales of Extraordinary Women

ELENA FAVILLI AND FRANCESCA CAVALLO

PARTICULAR BOOKS

an imprint of

PENGUIN BOOKS

PARTICULAR BOOKS

UK | USA | Canada | Ireland | Australia
India | New Zealand | South Africa

Particular Books is part of the Penguin Random House group of companies
whose addresses can be found at global.penguinrandomhouse.com.

First published in the United States of America by Timbuktu Labs, Inc. 2016
First published in Great Britain by Particular Books 2017
017

This is a work of creative nonfiction. It is a collection of heartwarming and thought-provoking
bedtime stories inspired by the life and adventures of one hundred heroic women. It is not an
encyclopedic account of events and accomplishments of their lives.

Editorial Direction & Art Direction by Francesca Cavallo and Elena Favilli

Printed in Italy by Graphicom

A CIP catalogue record for this book is available from the British Library

ISBN: 978–0–141–98600–5

www.greenpenguin.co.uk

MIX
Paper from
responsible sources
FSC® C018179

Penguin Random House is committed to a
sustainable future for our business, our readers
and our planet. This book is made from Forest
Stewardship Council® certified paper.

To the rebel girls of the world:

Dream bigger

Aim higher

Fight harder

And, when in doubt, remember

You are right.

· CONTENTS ·

• PREFACE •

There are many reasons why this book will always be special to us. Some are obvious: the record-breaking amount of money we raised through crowdfunding (more than one million dollars! *Good Night Stories for Rebel Girls* is the most funded original book in the history of crowdfunding), the astonishing number of backers from more than seventy countries, and the privilege of working with dozens of unbelievably talented female artists from all over the world.

Some reasons, though, are less obvious: the messages of soon-to-be moms and dads who told us that this is the first book they have bought for their daughters. The friend of a friend who said that this campaign gave her the confidence to start working on a project close to her heart that she had kept on hold for a long time because "what if I fail?" The email from a mom ecstatic to have a book that could help her share her perspective on the world with her three sons, not only as a mother, but as a woman. Above all, the deep trust that our backers have put in us.

This amount of trust is not something women get to experience very often. We do not take it for granted. How could we? Most of the extraordinary women featured in this book never experienced this kind of trust. No matter the importance of their discoveries, the audacity of their adventures, the width of their genius—they were constantly belittled, forgotten, in some cases almost erased from history.

It is important that girls understand the obstacles that lie in front of them. It is just as important that they know these obstacles are not insurmountable. That not only can they find a way to overcome them, but that they can remove those obstacles for those who will come after them, just like these great women did.

Each of the hundred stories in this book proves the world-changing power of a trusting heart.

May these brave pioneers inspire you. May their portraits impress upon our daughters the solid belief that beauty manifests itself in all shapes and colors, and at all ages. May each reader know the greatest success is to live a life full of passion, curiosity, and generosity. May we all remember every day that we have the right to be happy and to explore wildly.

Now that you're holding this book, all we can feel is hope and enthusiasm for the world we're building together. A world where gender will not define how big you can dream, how far you can go. A world where each of us will be able to say with confidence: "I am free."

Thank you for being part of this journey.

Elena Favilli
Francesca Cavallo

GOOD NIGHT STORIES FOR REBEL GIRLS

ADA LOVELACE

MATHEMATICIAN

Once upon a time, there was a girl named Ada who loved machines.

She also loved the idea of flying.

She studied birds to work out the perfect balance between wing size and body weight. She tested out materials and tried out several designs. She never managed to soar like a bird, but she created a beautiful book full of drawings called *Flyology* where she recorded all of her findings.

One night, Ada went to a ball. There, she met a grumpy old mathematician named Charles Babbage. Ada was a brilliant mathematician herself, and the two soon became good friends. Charles invited Ada to see a machine he had invented. He called it the *Difference Engine*. It could automatically add and subtract numbers. No one had ever done that before.

Ada was hooked.

"What if we built a machine that could make more complicated calculations?" she said. Excited, Ada and Charles started working. The machine was huge and it required an enormous steam engine.

Ada wanted to go further: "What if this machine could play music and show letters as well as numbers?"

She was describing a computer, way before modern computers were invented!

Ada wrote the first computer program in history.

DECEMBER 10, 1815–NOVEMBER 27, 1852
UNITED KINGDOM

"THAT BRAIN OF MINE IS
SOMETHING MORE THAN MERELY
MORTAL, AS TIME WILL SHOW."
—ADA LOVELACE

· ALEK WEK ·

SUPERMODEL

Once upon a time, there was a girl named Alek who would stop by a mango tree to get a snack on her way home from school.

In Alek's village, there was no running water nor electricity. She had to walk to a well for drinking water, but she and her family lived a simple and happy life.

Then, a terrible war broke out and Alek's life changed forever. As the warning sirens wailed over their village, Alek and her family had to run away from the fighting.

It was the rainy season. The river had flooded, the bridges across it were underwater, and Alek could not swim. She was terrified of drowning, but her mom helped her to cross safely to the other side. Along the way, Alek's mom traded packets of salt for food and passports because they didn't have any money. They managed to escape from the war, and made their way to London.

One day, she was in a park when a talent scout from a famous modeling agency approached her. He wanted to recruit Alek as a model. Alek's mother did not want to hear about it. But the agent persisted, and she finally agreed.

Alek looked so different from any other model, that she instantly became a sensation.

Alek wants every girl on the planet to know, "You are beautiful. It's okay to be quirky, it's fine to be shy. You don't have to go with the crowd."

BORN APRIL 16, 1977

SUDAN

ILLUSTRATION BY
BIJOU KARMAN

"WHEN BEAUTY SHINES
FROM WITHIN, THERE
CAN BE NO DENYING IT."
—ALEK WEK

ALFONSINA STRADA

CYCLIST

Once there was a girl who could ride a bike so fast that you could barely see her. "Don't go so fast, Alfonsina!" her parents would scream. Too late—she had already whizzed past.

When she got married, her family hoped that she would finally give up this crazy idea of becoming a cyclist. Instead, on her wedding day, her husband gifted her a brand-new racing bike. They moved to Milan, and Alfonsina started to train professionally.

She was so fast and so strong that a few years later, she entered the Giro d'Italia, one of the toughest races in the world. No other woman had ever attempted it before. "She'll never make it," people said. But nobody could stop Alfonsina.

The race was long and strenuous, with twenty-one day-long stages along some of the steepest mountain roads in Europe. Of the ninety cyclists who started out, only thirty made it across the finish line: Alfonsina was one of them. She was greeted as a hero.

The next year, she was barred from competing. "Giro d'Italia is a men's race," the officials declared. But that didn't stop her either.

She raced all the same and she set a speed record that stood for twenty-six years, even though she rode a 44-pound, 1-gear bike!

She would be happy to know that things have changed a lot since then. Now, women's cycle racing is hugely popular. It's even an Olympic sport.

MARCH 16, 1891–SEPTEMBER 13, 1959
ITALY

"NOBODY CAN
STOP MY BIKE."
—ALFONSINA STRADA

ALICIA ALONSO

BALLERINA

Once upon a time, there was a blind girl who became a great ballerina.

Her name was Alicia.

Alicia grew up sighted, and was already a wonderful ballerina with a great career ahead of her, when she fell ill. Her eyesight got worse and worse. She was forced to stay in bed for months without moving, but Alicia had to dance—so she danced in the only way she could: "I danced in my mind. Blinded, motionless, flat on my back, I taught myself to dance *Giselle*."

One day, the New York City Ballet's prima ballerina injured herself. They called Alicia to step in. She was already partially blind but how could she say no? The ballet was *Giselle*!

As soon as she started to dance, the audience fell in love with her.

Alicia danced with grace and confidence even though she could barely see. She trained her partners to be exactly where she needed them at just the right time.

Her style was so unique that she was asked to dance with her ballet company all over the world. But her dream was to bring classical ballet to Cuba, her home country.

Back from her travels, she started to teach classical ballet to Cuban dancers. She founded the Alicia Alonso Ballet Company, which later became the Ballet Nacional De Cuba.

BORN DECEMBER 21, 1921
CUBA

"A DANCER SHOULD LEARN
FROM ALL THE ARTS."
—ALICIA ALONSO

AMEENAH GURIB-FAKIM

PRESIDENT AND SCIENTIST

In an island nation in the Indian Ocean called Mauritius, there lived a girl who wanted to know everything about plants. Her name was Ameenah. Ameenah studied biodiversity.

She analyzed hundreds of aromatic and medicinal herbs and flowers. She studied their properties and travelled to rural villages to learn from traditional healers how they used plants in their rituals.

For Ameenah, plants were like friends.

Her favorite tree was the baobab because it is so useful: It stores water in its trunk, its leaves can cure infections, and its fruit (called *monkey apple*) contains more proteins than human milk.

Ameenah thought that a lot could be learned from plants. Plants, like benjoin, for example: "The leaves of benjoin are different shapes and sizes. Animals won't eat plants they don't recognize. So they tend to leave this plant alone. Quite smart, don't you think?"

Ameenah thought of plants as living, biological labs, full of vital information for humans and every other species. "Every time a forest is cut down, we lose an entire laboratory. A lab that we will never, ever recover."

Ameenah Gurib was elected President of Mauritius and every day she fights hard for all the inhabitants of her country: people, animals and, of course, plants.

OCTOBER 17, 1959
MAURITIUS

"HUMBLE PLANTS HIDE
SURPRISING SECRETS."
—AMEENAH GURIB-FAKIM

AMELIA EARHART

AVIATOR

Once upon a time, a girl called Amelia saved enough money to buy a yellow airplane.

She called it The Canary.

A few years later, she became the first woman to fly solo across the Atlantic Ocean. It was a dangerous flight. Her tiny plane was tossed around by strong winds and icy storms. She kept herself going with a can of tomato juice, sucked through a straw. After almost fifteen hours she touched down in a field in Northern Ireland, much to the surprise of the cows. "Have you come far?" the farmer asked her. "All the way from America!" she laughed.

Amelia loved to fly and she loved to do things no one had ever done before.

Her biggest challenge was to be the first woman to fly around the world.

She could only take a small bag, as all the space in the plane had to be used for fuel. Her long flight was going well. She was supposed to land on the tiny Howland Island, but never got there. In her last transmission, Amelia said she was flying through clouds and was running low on fuel. Her plane disappeared somewhere over the Pacific Ocean and was never found.

Before leaving, she wrote, "I am quite aware of the hazards. I want to do it, because I want to do it. Women must try to do the same things that men have tried. If they fail, their failure must be a challenge to others."

JULY 24, 1897–CA. JULY 1937
UNITED STATES OF AMERICA

ILLUSTRATION BY
GIULIA FLAMINI

"ADVENTURE IS
WORTHWHILE IN ITSELF."
—AMELIA EARHART

AMNA AL HADDAD

WEIGHTLIFTER

Once upon a time, there was a journalist named Amna. Amna was not happy. She was overweight and unfit. One day, she said to herself: "You can do much more than this. Just do something. Go for a walk."

And that's what she did.

She enjoyed her walks so much she wanted to do more. She ran long distances. She sprinted. She started to work out at the gym; when she discovered weightlifting she knew this was the sport for her.

Amna's life changed when the International Weightlifting Federation allowed Muslim women to compete in a unitard (an outfit that covers all skin). She started competing in Europe and America and became an icon for Muslim girls across the world.

"I like being strong," says Amna. "Being a girl does not mean you can't be as strong as a boy, or even stronger!"

She liked weightlifting so much that she started training for the Olympic games in Rio.

She thinks everyone should find a sport they like, and practice it. "Whatever your age, religion, or ethnicity, sport is good for everyone," she says. "It creates peace and it unites nations."

"No matter what the challenges are, never walk away from your dream. The more you persist, the closer you are going to get to your goals. When things get tough, just get tougher."

BORN OCTOBER 21, 1989
UNITED ARAB EMIRATES

"NOBODY CAN TELL ME WHAT
I CAN AND CANNOT DO."
—AMNA AL HADDAD

ANN MAKOSINSKI

Once there was a girl who couldn't study when it was dark because her house didn't have electricity. One day, her friend Ann came to visit and together they talked about the issue.

Ann was great at building things and she was especially passionate about transistors, devices that regulate the flow of electric current.

"What if I could invent a flashlight that is powered by your body?" Ann asked her friend. "After all, our bodies give off lots of energy in the form of heat."

The girls got very excited.

"Just think how many people could have electricity if this worked!"

Ann was just fifteen years old but she already had a lot of experience taking things apart and putting them back together.

So she started to work on this mysterious new flashlight. She called it the Hollow Flashlight because she built it using a hollow aluminum tube.

When she presented it to the Google Science Fair, she won first prize! It's the first flashlight that doesn't need batteries, wind, or sun: just body heat.

Today Ann is considered one of the most promising inventors of our time.

Her dream is to make Hollow Flashlights available for free to everyone in the world who can't afford electricity.

"I like the idea of using technology to make the world a better place and to keep our environment clean," she always says.

BORN OCTOBER 3, 1997
CANADA

ILLUSTRATION BY
CLAUDIA CARIERI

"IF YOU ARE ALIVE, YOU
PRODUCE SOME LIGHT."
—ANN MAKOSINSKI

ANNA POLITKOVSKAYA

JOURNALIST

Once upon a time, in Russia, many books were forbidden. Some of these were by writers that a little girl called Anna loved. Anna's parents used to smuggle in her favorite books so she could read to her heart's content.

Anna grew up and became a journalist.

When a part of Russia called Chechnya wanted to break away and become an independent nation, the Russian government sent in troops to stop them. A brutal war broke out. Anna decided that she had to write. She wanted to tell the world what was really happening in Chechnya. The Russian government did not like that at all.

"Why are you putting your life at risk?" Anna's husband once asked her. "Risk is part of my profession," she answered. "I know that something may happen to me. I just want my articles to make the world better."

Many bad things happened, but Anna was brave.

Once, she had to run all night long in the Chechen hills to escape from the Russian Security Services. People on both sides wanted to stop her from telling the truth—someone even put poison in her tea to try and get rid of her. But despite these dangers, she bravely carried on telling the truth about everything she saw.

Anna continued to risk her life until she died, writing the truth in order to make the world a better place.

AUGUST 30, 1958–OCTOBER 7, 2006
RUSSIA

ILLUSTRATION BY
LEA HEINRICH

"WHAT MATTERS IS THE
INFORMATION, NOT WHAT
YOU THINK ABOUT IT."
ANNA POLITKOVSKAYA

· ARTEMISIA GENTILESCHI ·

PAINTER

Once there was a girl who was an amazing painter. Her name was Artemisia and she was beautiful and strong.

Her father, Orazio, was also a painter and trained her in his studio from the time she was little.

By the time she was seventeen years old, Artemisia had already painted several masterpieces. Yet, people were skeptical about her. "How can she paint like this?" they whispered to each other.

At that time, most women were not even allowed to get close to famous artists' studios.

One day, her father asked his friend, the famous painter Agostino Tassi, to teach Artemisia perspective, how to create a three-dimensional space on a flat surface.

Agostino wanted his star pupil to also be his lover. "I promise I will marry you," he told her. Artemisia kept saying no.

Things became so bad that Artemisia finally told her father what was going on. Artemisia's father believed her, and even though Agostino was a powerful man and a dangerous enemy, Orazio took him to court.

During the trial, Agostino denied doing anything wrong. Artemisia faced terrible pressure but stuck to the truth and didn't give in. In the end, Agostino was found guilty. Today, Artemisia is considered one of the greatest painters of all times.

JULY 8, 1593–JUNE 14, 1653

ITALY

ILLUSTRATION BY
MONICA GARWOOD

"AS LONG AS I LIVE, I WILL HAVE
CONTROL OVER MY BEING."
—ARTEMISIA GENTILESCHI

· ASHLEY FIOLEK ·

MOTOCROSS RACER

A little girl called Ashley was playing in the kitchen when some pans fell off the table with a massive crash. Ashley didn't even turn around. Her mom and dad decided to get her hearing tested. When the results came back, they found out that their daughter was deaf.

They learned sign language and sent Ashley to camp with other deaf kids so she could learn from them and build up her self-confidence.

Ashley's father and her grandfather loved motorcycles, so they gave her a peewee motorbike when she was three. The three of them would head to the woods, each of them on their own motorcycle. Ashley loved these outings and she started dreaming about becoming a motocross racer.

Most people told her it was impossible. "Hearing is really important in motocross," they said. "The sound of the engine tells you when to shift gears. You have to be able to hear where the other riders are."

But Ashley could feel from the engine's vibration when to change gears. She looked for shadows in the corner of her eye and knew when someone was getting close.

In five years she won four national titles. She fell, many times! Ashley broke her left arm, her right wrist, her right ankle, her collarbone (three times) and her two front teeth, but she always recovered and got back on her bike.

Ashley has a pickup truck parked in her driveway. On the back, a bumper sticker reads: "Honk all you want, I'm deaf!"

BORN OCTOBER 22, 1990
UNITED STATES OF AMERICA

ILLUSTRATION BY
KATE PRIOR

"I DON'T THINK ABOUT VIBRATIONS; I DON'T THINK ABOUT ANYTHING AT ALL. I'M PART OF THE BIKE NOW."
—ASHLEY FIOLEK

ASTRID LINDGREN

WRITER

Once there was a girl who lived on a farm with her big family. She would spend entire days roaming free in the fields with her brothers and sisters, but she also helped take care of the farm animals. Not just the small ones like chickens and ducks—even the big ones like cows and horses!

Her name was Astrid and she had quite a rebellious spirit.

She was strong, brave, never scared of being alone, and she could do all sorts of things: clean, cook, fix a bike, walk along rooftops, fight off bullies, make up fantastic stories . . . Sound familiar? Well, if you've ever read about another little girl who was strong, brave, and fearless called Pippi Longstocking, you won't be surprised to learn that Astrid was the author of that brilliant book.

When *Pippi Longstocking* was published, lots of adults disapproved. "Pippi is too rebellious," they said. "Our children will think being disobedient is okay." Children, on the other hand, absolutely loved it. Pippi didn't just say *no* without any reason: she showed young readers the importance of being independent, while always caring for others.

Today *Pippi Longstocking* is the one of the best-loved books in children's literature. Astrid went on to write and publish many more books, always depicting strong children in charge of their own adventures.

So, whenever you're in trouble for something you did, grab a copy of *Pippi Longstocking*. She will always be there to help you!

NOVEMBER 14, 1907–JANUARY 28, 2002
SWEDEN

ILLUSTRATION BY
JUSTINE LECOUFFE

"MISCHIEF ISN'T
SOMETHING YOU THINK
UP. IT JUST HAPPENS."
—ASTRID LINDGREN

AUNG SAN SUU KYI

POLITICIAN

Once there was a young woman named Suu Kyi. She came from a rich Burmese family who traveled the world.

Suu Kyi, her husband, and their two children were living in England when the phone rang.

"My mom has fallen ill," she said to her children. "I have to go back home to take care of her."

She planned to stay there for a few weeks, but from the moment she landed, she found herself involved in protests against a military dictator. He had taken over the country and he imprisoned anyone who opposed him.

Suu Kyi spoke out against him and quickly got lots of support. The dictator realized that this young woman was a powerful threat. He gave her a tough choice: "You are free to leave the country and never come back. Or you can stay, a prisoner in your own home."

Suu Kyi thought about it. She very much wanted to rejoin her husband and children in England, but she knew her people needed her. "I'll stay," she said.

Suu Kyi spent most of the next twenty-one years as a prisoner in her own home. She met people there, spoke about her beliefs, and spread her message of democracy and peaceful change. She won the Nobel Peace Prize, and inspired millions of people in her own country and across the world, all without leaving her house.

After being finally released, she was elected leader of her country.

BORN JUNE 19, 1945

BURMA

ILLUSTRATION BY
LIZZY STEWART

"SINCE WE LIVE IN
THIS WORLD, WE HAVE
TO DO OUR BEST FOR
THIS WORLD."
—AUNG SAN SUU KYI

BALKISSA CHAIBOU

ACTIVIST

Once there was a girl who wanted to become a doctor. Her name was Balkissa and she was really good at school. One day, she discovered that her uncle had promised her in marriage to one of her cousins.

Balkissa was horrified. "You can't force me to get married! I want to be a doctor."

Unfortunately, the country where Balkissa lived allows parents to arrange weddings for their daughters when they are still children.

"Just let me stay in school five more years," Balkissa begged her parents.

Her parents agreed to postpone the marriage, but after five years, Balkissa's love of learning had only grown stronger. The night before her wedding, she escaped from her house and ran to the closest police station to ask for help. She decided to challenge her uncle in court.

She was terrified that this might turn her whole family against her, but her mother quietly encouraged her to keep fighting. The judge agreed with Balkissa, and when her uncle threatened her, he was forced to leave the country. "The day I won the case and I put my school uniform back on, I felt my life was renewed," she says.

Today, Balkissa is at university studying hard to become a doctor. She also campaigns for other young girls to follow her example and say 'no' to forced marriage. She visits schools and speaks to tribal chiefs about the issue.

"Study with all your might. It's not easy but it's your only hope," she says.

BORN 1995

NIGER

"I WILL SHOW THEM WHAT
I CAN DO WITH MY LIFE."
—BALKISSA CHAIBOU

BRENDA CHAPMAN

DIRECTOR

Once there was a girl who had curly red hair and loved to draw. Her name was Brenda.

When she was fifteen years old, Brenda called up Walt Disney Studios. "I'm really good at drawing," she said. "Will you give me a job?" They told her to get back in touch when she was older and had some training.

That's exactly what she did. She studied character animation at CalArts, and a few years later found herself exactly where she'd always dreamed: working on animated films for Disney in Los Angeles. She soon discovered that she was one of the very few women animators there.

"That's when I realized why princesses in their films were so helpless: They had all been created by men," she recalls. She promised herself that she would create a new type of princess: strong, independent, and . . .

". . . *Brave*," she thought. "What a great name for a film!"

Princess Merida in *Brave* is anything but helpless. She's a fantastic archer, and gallops around on her horse, fighting off bears and having amazing adventures. Brenda based the character on her own little girl, Emma—a strong, free-spirited girl, just like her mom! "She is my Merida . . . and I adore her."

Brenda won an Oscar and a Golden Globe for her film.

She also worked on many other award-winning films, like *Beauty and Beast*, *The Little Mermaid*, and *The Lion King*. Brenda became the first woman to direct an animated feature for a major Hollywood studio with *Prince of Egypt*.

BORN NOVEMBER 1, 1962
UNITED STATES OF AMERICA

"I DREW SINCE I WAS A
LITTLE KID—AND I WANTED
TO DRAW IN MY CAREER."
—BRENDA CHAPMAN

· THE BRONTË SISTERS ·

WRITERS

In a cold, bleak house in northern England, there once lived three sisters. Charlotte, Emily, and Anne were often alone and they wrote stories and poems to entertain themselves.

One day, Charlotte decided to send her poems to a famous English poet to ask what he thought of them. His response was, "I do not like your poems at all: literature is a man's business!"

Charlotte kept on writing.

One night, she found a notebook lying open on Emily's desk. "Why have you not shown us your poems before?" Charlotte asked. "They are beautiful." Emily was furious at her sister reading her private papers without her permission. But once Emily calmed down, Charlotte proposed: "Why don't we write a book of poetry together?" Emily and Anne agreed.

When they finally published the book, it only sold two copies. But they still did not give up and they kept working in secret, discussing their writing at the dinner table.

This time, they each worked on a different novel. When the novels came out, they were hugely successful. People at the time couldn't believe that they had been written by three country girls, so the sisters had to travel to London to prove that they were indeed the authors.

Their books have been translated into many different languages and read by millions of people across the world.

CA. 1816–CA. 1855
UNITED KINGDOM

ILLUSTRATION BY
ELISABETTA STOINICH

"I AM NOT AN ANGEL, AND I
WILL NOT BE ONE TILL I DIE:
I WILL BE MYSELF."
—CHARLOTTE BRONTË

· CATHERINE THE GREAT ·

EMPRESS

Once there was a queen who disliked her husband.

Her name was Catherine and her husband, Peter, was the emperor of Russia. The Russian people found him mean and arrogant.

Catherine knew she would do a better job of ruling the country. All she had to do was to figure out a way of replacing her husband.

Six months after becoming emperor, Peter went on vacation, leaving Catherine behind. This was her chance. Catherine gave a rousing speech to the royal soldiers to get them on her side. They switched their loyalty from Peter to Catherine, and a priest declared her the new ruler of Russia. She then ordered a suitably magnificent crown to be made.

Almost the first thing she did as empress was to order her husband to be arrested and put in jail.

Catherine's magnificent crown took two months to create! It was made of gold and silver encrusted with 4,936 diamonds, 75 pearls, and a huge ruby on top.

During her reign, Catherine expanded the Russian empire, winning many wars and uprisings.

Lots of people were envious of this powerful woman. They said nasty things about her behind her back when she was alive, and when she died, they said she must have fallen off the toilet! In fact, she died in her bed and was buried in a sumptuous golden tomb in Peter and Paul Cathedral in Saint Petersburg.

MAY 2, 1729–NOVEMBER 17, 1796
RUSSIA

"I AM ONE OF THE
PEOPLE WHO LOVE
THE WHY OF THINGS."
—CATHERINE THE GREAT

CHOLITA CLIMBERS

Once upon a time, at the foot of a beautiful mountain in Bolivia, there lived a woman called Lydia Huayllas.

All her life, Lydia and her friends had cooked for mountaineers before they set off from base camps to climb the mountain. She used to watch them put on their helmets, strap on their backpacks, tighten their boots, and fill their water bottles. She saw the excited looks in their eyes.

Lydia and the other women did not know what it was like on top of the mountain. Their husbands did and their sons did. It was their job to act as mountain guides and porters, taking groups of climbers safely up to the peaks and back down again while the women stayed at camp, in the valley.

One day, Lydia said: "Let's go up and see for ourselves."

As the women pulled on their boots and crampons under their colorful skirts (*cholitas*), the men laughed. "You can't wear cholitas," they said. "You have to wear proper climbing gear."

"Nonsense," Lydia said, strapping on her hardhat. "We can wear what we like. We are the cholita climbers!"

Through snowstorms and high winds, the women climbed peak after peak. "We are strong. We want to climb eight mountains," they said.

As you read this, they are probably tramping through the snow, the wind swirling their multi-colored skirts, filled with the excitement of seeing the world from yet another peak.

BORN CA. 1968
BOLIVIA

"BEING ON THE TOP IS WONDERFUL.
IT'S ANOTHER WORLD."
—LYDIA HUAYLLAS

CLAUDIA RUGGERINI

PARTISAN

Once there was a girl who had to change her name. "Hey, Marisa!" her friends would call out. Nobody could know that her real name was Claudia: It was too dangerous.

Claudia lived at a time when Italy was ruled by a tyrannical man called Benito Mussolini. During Mussolini's dictatorship, you couldn't read certain books, you couldn't watch certain movies, you couldn't express your opinion, and you couldn't vote.

Claudia believed in freedom and decided to fight this man with all her strength, so she joined a group of partisans (*partigiani* in Italian) to help bring down the dictator.

Claudia's group was made up of young university students. They would meet in secret after class to bring out their own newspaper. But how could they spread their message with Mussolini's police everywhere?

Claudia was incredibly brave. She cycled around delivering newspapers and messages from one secret location to another for almost two years. One day, the regime finally collapsed. The national radio announced that Italy was free from fascism and people flooded onto the streets to celebrate.

Claudia—Marisa—had one last task. With a small group of partisans, she entered the offices of Italy's national newspaper, *Il Corriere della Sera*, and officially liberated it from censorship after twenty years. Finally, they were free to print the truth—and Claudia's friends could call her by her real name at last.

FEBRUARY 1922–JULY 4, 2016
ITALY

"STRONGER THAN FEAR IS THE
DESIRE TO FIGHT FOR FREEDOM."
—CLAUDIA RUGGERINI

· CLEOPATRA ·

PHARAOH

Once upon a time, in ancient Egypt, a pharaoh died and left his kingdom to his ten-year-old son, Ptolemy XIII and to his eighteen-year-old daughter Cleopatra.

The two had such different ideas on how to run the country that soon Cleopatra was kicked out of the palace and a civil war broke out.

Julius Caesar, the emperor of Rome, traveled to Egypt to help Cleopatra and Ptolemy find an agreement. "If only I could meet Caesar before my brother does," Cleopatra thought "I could convince him that I'm the better pharaoh." But she had been banished from the Palace. The guards would have blocked her at the entrance.

Cleopatra asked her servants to roll her up inside a carpet and to smuggle her into Caesar's rooms. Impressed by her daring, Caesar restored Cleopatra to the throne. They became a couple and had a son. Cleopatra moved to Rome but then Caesar was killed, so she went back to Egypt.

The new Roman leader, Marc Antony, had heard a lot about this strong Egyptian queen and wanted to meet her. This time, she arrived on a golden barge, surrounded by precious jewels and silk.

It was love at first sight.

Cleopatra and Marc Antony were inseparable. They had three children and loved each other to the end of their lives.

When Cleopatra died, the empire ended with her. She was the last pharaoh to rule Ancient Egypt.

69 B.C.–AUGUST 12, 30 B.C.

EGYPT

ILLUSTRATION BY
KIKI LJUNG

"I WILL NOT BE
TRIUMPHED
OVER."
—CLEOPATRA

• COCO CHANEL •

FASHION DESIGNER

Once upon a time, in central France, there was a girl who lived in a convent, surrounded by nuns dressed in black and white. Her name was Gabrielle Chanel.

In the convent, girls were taught how to sew, but they didn't have many colors to choose from. They used the same material as nuns did, so all their dolls were dressed in black and white, too!

When she grew up, Gabrielle worked as a seamstress by day and a singer by night. The soldiers she sang for at the bar called her *Coco*, and the nickname would stick with her for the rest of her life.

Coco dreamed of having her own shop in Paris. One day, a wealthy friend of hers lent her enough money to make her dream come true.

Coco's clothes looked fabulous, even if the cloth was plain. "Where did you buy that?" the chic Parisian ladies would ask her. "I made it myself," she'd say, "Come to my shop and I can make one for you, too."

Business grew quickly and Coco soon repaid all the money to her friend.

Her most successful design was her classic "little black dress." She transformed the color that had always been associated with funerals to something perfect for a glamorous evening out.

The shape of many of the clothes we wear today was heavily influenced by Coco Chanel, the designer who started life making doll's clothes from scraps of nuns' skirts.

AUGUST 19, 1883–JANUARY 10, 1971
FRANCE

"SOME PEOPLE
THINK THAT
LUXURY IS THE
OPPOSITE OF
POVERTY. IT IS
NOT. IT'S THE
OPPOSITE OF
VULGARITY."
—COCO CHANEL

CORA CORALINA

POET AND BAKER

Once upon a time, in a house on a bridge, there was a little girl named Cora who knew she was a poet.

Her family did not think so. They did not want her to read books and they did not want to send her to high school. They thought her job was to find a good husband and raise a family.

When she grew up, Cora fell in love with a man and they got married. She moved with him to the big city and they had four children. She worked at all sorts of jobs to make sure her children could go to school.

Cora had a busy life, but she never forgot she was a poet. She wrote every single day.

When she was sixty years old, she moved back to the house on the bridge. She decided it was time to start her career as a poet. Cora still needed money, so she baked cakes to sell on her doorstep along with her poems.

Cora's poems started to be appreciated by other poets and writers. She won prizes and medals and—when she was seventy-five years old—she published her very first book.

Journalists came from all over the country to interview her while she was baking. And when they left, she sat back down at her desk and started to write again, surrounded by the delicious smells of pies, cookies, and cakes.

AUGUST 20, 1889–APRIL 10, 1985
BRAZIL

"I'M THAT WOMAN WHO
CLIMBED THE MOUNTAIN OF
LIFE, REMOVING STONES AND
PLANTING FLOWERS."
—CORA CORALINA

· COY MATHIS ·

ELEMENTARY SCHOOL STUDENT

Once upon a time, a boy named Coy was born. Coy loved dresses, the color pink, and shiny shoes.

Coy wanted his parents to address him as "she" and didn't like wearing boys' clothes. His parents let him wear whatever he liked.

One night, Coy asked his mom, "When are we going to the doctor to have me fixed into a girl-girl?"

The doctor explained: "Usually, boys feel OK with being boys, and girls are fine with being girls. But there are some boys who feel female, and girls who feel male. They're called transgender, and Coy is a transgender girl. She was born in a boy's body but, deep inside, she feels that she's a girl and she should be allowed to be one."

From then on, Coy's mom and dad asked everyone to treat Coy as a girl.

But when school started, they had an unexpected problem. "Coy has to either use the boys' bathroom, or the bathroom for disabled children," the teachers said.

"But I'm not a boy!" Coy wailed. "And I'm not disabled! I'm a girl."

Coy's parents talked to a judge about the situation.

The judge thought about it and decided: "Coy should be allowed to use whichever bathroom she wants."

Coy and her parents threw a big party to celebrate. They ate pink cake, and Coy wore a sparkly pink dress and beautiful pink shoes.

BORN CA. 2007
UNITED STATES OF AMERICA

"I WANT TO GO TO SCHOOL.
WE PLAY GAMES AT RECESS."
—COY MATHIS

ELIZABETH I

Once upon a time, there was a king who wanted to leave his kingdom to a son.

When his wife gave birth to a daughter, King Henry VIII was so mad that he left her, sent the child away, and married another woman. He believed that only a man would be able to rule the country after he died, and was delighted when his new wife gave birth to a boy: Edward.

Henry's daughter, Elizabeth, grew up a bright and brilliant girl, with striking red hair and a fiery temper.

Edward was only nine when his father died and he became King. A few years later, he also became ill and died, and his sister Mary became queen. Mary thought that Elizabeth was plotting against her, so she locked Elizabeth up in the Tower of London.

One day, the Tower guards burst into her cell. "The Queen is dead," they announced. And then they fell to their knees in front of her. Elizabeth instantly went from being a prisoner in the Tower to the country's new queen.

Elizabeth's court was home to musicians, poets, painters, and playwrights. The most famous was William Shakespeare, whose plays Elizabeth adored. She wore sumptuous gowns decorated with pearls and lace. She never married: She valued her own independence as highly as that of her country.

Her people loved her dearly and, when she died, Londoners took the streets to mourn the greatest queen they had ever had.

SEPTEMBER 7, 1533–MARCH 24, 1603
UNITED KINGDOM

"A CLEAR AND INNOCENT
CONSCIENCE FEARS
NOTHING."
—ELIZABETH I

EUFROSINA CRUZ

ACTIVIST AND POLITICIAN

Once there was a girl who didn't want to make tortillas. When her father told her that women can only make tortillas and children, she burst into tears and promised to show him that it wasn't true. "You can leave this house, but don't expect a single cent from me," he told her.

Eufrosina started out by selling chewing gum and fruit on the street to pay for her studies. She got a degree in accounting and came back home with a job as a teacher. She started to teach young indigenous girls like herself, so they could also find the strength and the resources to build their own lives.

One day, she decided to run for mayor of her town. She won many votes, but despite that, the townsmen canceled the election. "A woman as mayor? Don't be ridiculous," they said. Furious, Eufrosina started to work even harder. She founded an organization called QUIEGO, to help indigenous women fight for their rights. Their symbol was a white lily. "Wherever I go, I take this flower to remind people that indigenous women are exactly like that: natural, beautiful, and resilient," Eufrosina said.

A few years later, Eufrosina became the first indigenous woman to be elected president of the state congress. When the first lady of Mexico came to visit, Eufrosina walked arm-in-arm with her, in front of the local population.

She showed her father—and the whole world—that there is nothing that the strong, indigenous women of Mexico cannot do.

BORN JANUARY 1, 1979
MEXICO

"WHEN A WOMAN DECIDES TO CHANGE, EVERYTHING CHANGES AROUND HER."
—EUFROSINA CRUZ

ILLUSTRATION BY
PAOLA ROLLO

EVITA PERÓN

POLITICIAN

Once upon a time, in South America, lived a beautiful girl called Eva. As a child, Eva dreamed of escaping her life of poverty by becoming a famous actress and film star.

When she was just fifteen years old, Eva moved to the big city of Buenos Aires to pursue her dream. With her talent, good looks, and determination, she soon became a celebrated actress onstage and on the radio. But Eva wanted more: She wanted to help people less fortunate than herself.

One night, at a party, she met Colonel Juan Perón, a powerful politician. They fell in love and got married shortly after.

When Juan Perón was elected President of Argentina one year later, Eva quickly became known by her affectionate nickname: Evita. The people loved her passion and her commitment to helping the poor. She fought hard for women's rights and helped women win their right to vote.

She became such a legendary figure that she was asked to run as vice president to help govern alongside her husband. Although she was loved by the poor, many powerful people feared her charisma and power. "They just can't deal with a young, successful woman," she used to say.

After discovering she had a serious illness, Evita decided not to run, although she did help her husband win a second term as president. When she died, only a few months later, the announcement came on national radio: "We have lost the spiritual chief of our nation."

MAY 7, 1919–JULY 26, 1952

ARGENTINA

ILLUSTRATION BY
CRISTINA AMODEO

"YOU MUST WANT! YOU
HAVE THE RIGHT TO ASK!
YOU MUST DESIRE."
—EVITA PERON

· FADUMO DAYIB ·

POLITICIAN

Once there was a girl whose childhood was spent trying to escape from war. Fadumo and her family had to stay one step ahead of the fighting, and she could not go to school. She did not learn to read and write until she was fourteen.

One day her mother told her, "You must leave the country. Take your brother and sister and go!" Fadumo knew that her mother was right: war-torn Somalia was one of the most dangerous places in the world for children.

When they finally arrived in Finland, they could do all the things that children can do when they live in a peaceful, democratic country. They had a home and beds. They had food every day. They could play, and go to school. They were never beaten, and they could see a doctor for free if they were ill.

But Fadumo never forgot about Somalia.

She wanted to learn everything she could so she could go back to her own country and help her people regain freedom and peace. After earning three master's degrees, she left her family in Finland and started to work with the United Nations to set up hospitals across Somalia.

"I have to be there," she told her husband.

Today, Fadumo is Somalia's first female presidential candidate. No Somali woman has ever run for president before because it's extremely dangerous. But Fadumo has no doubts: "My mother always told me, 'You hold all life's possibilities in the palm of your hands.' And that's true."

BORN 1973
SOMALIA

ILLUSTRATION BY
LEA HEINRICH

"WE WILL NO LONGER NEGOTIATE
FOR OUR EXISTENCE."
—FADUMO DAYIB

FLORENCE NIGHTINGALE

NURSE

Once upon a time, a baby was born to an English couple travelling in Italy. They decided to name their daughter after the beautiful city where she was born, so they called her Florence.

Florence loved traveling, she loved math and science, and she loved collecting information. Whenever she traveled to a new place, she would note down how many people lived there, how many hospitals there were, and how big the city was.

She loved numbers.

Florence studied nursing and became so good at it that the government sent her to manage a hospital for injured soldiers in Turkey.

As soon as she arrived, Florence started collecting and examining all the data she could find. She discovered that most of the soldiers died not because of their wounds, but because of infections and diseases contracted in the hospital.

"The very first requirement in a hospital is that it should do the sick no harm," she said.

She made sure that everyone working there washed their hands frequently and kept everything clean. At night, she carried a lamp as she made her rounds, talking to her patients and giving them hope.

Thanks to her, many more soldiers made it home safely, and she became known as "The Lady with the Lamp."

MAY 12, 1820–AUGUST 13, 1910
UNITED KINGDOM

"I ATTRIBUTE MY SUCCESS
TO THIS—I NEVER GAVE
OR TOOK ANY EXCUSE."
—FLORENCE NIGHTINGALE

FRIDA KAHLO

PAINTER

Once upon a time, in a bright blue house near Mexico City, lived a small girl called Frida. She would grow up to be one of the most famous painters of the twentieth century, but she almost didn't grow up at all.

When she was six, she nearly died from polio. The disease left her with a permanent limp, but that didn't stop her from playing, swimming, and wrestling just like all the other kids.

Then, when she was eighteen, she was involved in a terrible bus accident. She almost died again—and again she spent months in bed. Her mother made her a special easel so that she could paint while lying down, for more than anything else, Frida loved to paint.

As soon as she was able to walk again, she went to see Mexico's most famous artist, Diego Rivera. "Are my paintings any good?" she asked him. Her paintings were amazing: bold, bright, and beautiful. He fell in love with them—and he fell in love with Frida.

Diego and Frida got married. He was a big man in a large floppy hat. She looked tiny beside him. People called them "the elephant and the dove."

Frida painted hundreds of beautiful self-portraits during her life, often surrounded with the animals and birds that she kept. The bright blue house where she lived has been kept just as she left it, full of color and joy and flowers.

JULY 6, 1907–JULY 13, 1954
MEXICO

ILLUSTRATION BY
HELENA MORAIS SOARES

"FEET, WHAT DO I NEED
YOU FOR WHEN I HAVE
WINGS TO FLY?"
—FRIDA KAHLO

GRACE HOPPER

COMPUTER SCIENTIST

Once upon a time, there was a little girl called Grace who really wanted to understand how alarm clocks worked. She started taking apart all the clocks she could find. First one, then another, then the third....By the time she got to her seventh clock, her mom realized there were no more clocks in the house and told her to stop!

Grace kept tinkering with anything she found interesting. Eventually, she became a professor of math and physics. During the Second World War, she joined the Navy, like her grandfather who was an admiral.

She was assigned to work on a special project. "Come and meet Mark," they said. She went into a room but instead of a person, she was introduced to the first computer! Called "Mark I," it filled the entire room and—since it was the first—no one knew exactly how to use it. So Grace started studying it. It took a lot of hard work, but thanks to the programs Grace wrote for the Mark I and its successors, U.S. forces were able to decode secret messages sent by their enemies during the war.

When she was old, Grace tried to retire more than once, but she was always called back because of her extraordinary expertise. She eventually became an admiral like her grandfather.

All her life, Grace went to bed early and woke up at 5:00 a.m. to work on computer coding. She never stopped being curious and her incredible work showed the world what computers could do.

DECEMBER 9, 1906–JANUARY 1, 1992
UNITED STATES OF AMERICA

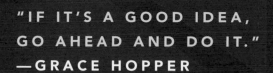

ILLUSTRATION BY
KIKI LJUNG

HOPPER

"IF IT'S A GOOD IDEA,
GO AHEAD AND DO IT."
—GRACE HOPPER

GRACE O'MALLEY

PIRATE

Once upon a time, on a wild green island, lived a girl with long ginger hair. Her name was Grace.

When wind howled and waves crashed against the rocks, Grace would stand on the clifftop and dream of sailing out across the stormy seas. "Girls cannot be sailors," her father told her. "And anyway, your long hair would get tangled in the rigging."

Grace didn't like this one bit. She cut her hair short and dressed in boy's clothes to prove to her family that she too could live the life of the sea.

Finally one day, her father agreed to take her sailing, on one condition: "If we meet a pirate ship, hide below deck," he said. But when they were attacked, Grace leaped off the rigging and landed on one of the pirates' backs! Her surprise attack worked—and they beat the pirates off.

Grace was a fine sailor, and wanted to do something more exciting than catching fish. When the English attacked her castle, she became a pirate herself rather than submit to English rule. Grace was so successful that soon she had her own fleet of ships as well as several islands and castles along the west coast of Ireland.

When the English captured her sons, Grace sailed to meet the Queen of England, Elizabeth I, to try and save them. To everyone's surprise, the queen and Grace became friends. The queen returned her sons and possessions, and Grace helped her fight against England's enemies, the Spanish.

CA. 1530–1603

IRELAND

ILLUSTRATION BY
KATHRIN HONESTA

"I AM THE QUEEN OF THE SEA."
—GRACE O'MALLEY

HARRIET TUBMAN

FREEDOM FIGHTER

One day, a girl was standing in front of a grocery store, when a black man came running past. He was being chased by a white man, who yelled, "Stop that man! He's my slave!"

She did nothing to stop him. The girl's name was Harriet, she was twelve years old—and she was also enslaved. Harriet hoped the man would escape. She wanted to help him.

Just then the overseer hurled an iron object at the running man. He missed, but hit Harriet on the head. She was badly injured but her thick hair cushioned the blow enough to save her life. "My hair had never been combed," she said, "and it stood out like a bushel basket."

A few years later, the family who owned her put her up for sale, so Harriet decided to escape.

She hid in the daytime and traveled by night. When she crossed the border into Pennsylvania, she realized for the first time in her life she was free. "I looked at my hands to see if I was the same person now that I was free. There was such glory over everything and I felt like I was in heaven."

She thought about the runaway slave, and her family in Maryland who were still enslaved. She knew she had to help them. Over the next eleven years, she went back nineteen times and rescued hundreds of enslaved people.

She was never captured, and she never lost a single person.

CA. 1822–MARCH 10, 1913
UNITED STATES OF AMERICA

ILLUSTRATION BY
SALLY NIXON

"...AND I PRAYED TO GOD TO MAKE
ME STRONG AND ABLE TO FIGHT,
AND THAT'S WHAT I'VE ALWAYS
PRAYED FOR EVER SINCE."
—HARRIET TUBMAN

· HATSHEPSUT ·

PHARAOH

Long before Cleopatra, a woman ruled Egypt for twenty-five years. Her name was Hatshepsut and she was the first woman to ever become pharaoh.

At the time, the idea of a woman being pharaoh was so strange that Hatshepsut had to act as though she was a man in order to convince Egyptians that she was their legitimate leader. She proclaimed herself *king* and not *queen* and canceled the female suffix in her name; she wore men's clothes and sometimes even put on a false beard!

Hatshepsut reigned longer and more successfully than any other pharaoh in all of Egyptian history. But apparently that wasn't enough. Twenty years after she died, someone tried to erase her from history. Statues of her were smashed, and her name was removed from the records.

Why? Because, a female pharaoh freaked people out. What if her success encouraged other women to seek power?

Thankfully, it's not so easy erase the memory of someone immortalized in stone.

Enough traces of her life and work remained for modern archeologists to piece together her story.

Hatshepsut's mummy, wrapped in linen and perfumed with resins, had been removed from her original grave and hidden, but it was found in the Valley of the Kings a few years ago.

CA. 1508–1458 B.C.

EGYPT

"I HAVE RESTORED THAT WHICH
WAS IN RUINS. I HAVE RAISED UP
THAT WHICH WAS DESTROYED."
—HATSHEPSUT

HELEN KELLER

ACTIVIST

Once upon a time, a girl named Helen suffered from a bad fever that left her deaf and blind. Frustrated and angry, she used to lie on the ground, kicking and screaming.

One day, her mom took Helen to a special school for the blind. A talented young teacher named Anne Sullivan met them and decided to try and teach Helen how to speak.

But how can you learn the word *doll* if you cannot see your doll, Anne wondered. How do you say *water* if you've never heard anyone speak?

Anne realized that she had to use Helen's sense of touch. She held Helen's fingers under running water, and spelled the word *water* on her hand. Then she spelled the word *doll* while Helen cuddled her favorite doll. Helen suddenly understood that different words stood for different things!

With her fingers on Anne's lips, Helen felt the vibrations when these words were spoken, and slowly she learned how to make those words herself. Soon, she was speaking out loud for the first time.

She learned how to read Braille by running her fingers over the raised dots. She even learned different languages: French, German, Latin, and Greek too!

Helen gave public speeches and championed the rights of people with disabilities. She traveled the world with her amazing teacher and her beloved dog. She didn't need words to tell them how she felt: she just gave them a big, loving hug.

JUNE 27, 1880–JUNE 1, 1968
UNITED STATES OF AMERICA

ILLUSTRATION BY
MONICA GARWOOD

"THE BEST AND MOST
BEAUTIFUL THINGS IN THE
WORLD CANNOT BE SEEN
OR EVEN TOUCHED—THEY
MUST BE FELT WITH THE
HEART."
—HELEN KELLER

HILLARY RODHAM CLINTON

PRESIDENTIAL CANDIDATE

There was a time when only boys could be whatever they wanted: baseball players, doctors, judges, policemen, presidents.

At that time, in Illinois, a girl named Hillary was born.

Hillary was a brave, blonde girl with thick glasses and boundless curiosity. She wanted to go out and explore the world, but she was scared of the rough boys in her neighborhood who laughed at her and called her names.

Once, her mother saw her hiding inside. "Hillary, you get out there and deal with them. Otherwise, the bullies will win without even a fight."

So out she went. She learned how to fight against bullies and soon found others who were fighting too: people of color fighting against racism, single moms fighting to bring up their kids. Hillary listened to all their stories, and tried to figure out how she could help.

The best way to fight for justice, she decided, was to go into politics. Because many Americans were not used to seeing a woman politician, they criticized her for silly reasons, like her hairstyle, the sound of her voice, or the clothes she wore. They tried to bully her out of politics. But Hillary had learned how to deal with bullies, and she stood up to them.

Hillary became the first woman nominated by a major party for President of the United States.

There was a time when girls could not be whatever they wanted, but that time is gone.

BORN OCTOBER 26, 1947
UNITED STATES OF AMERICA

"TO EVERY LITTLE GIRL WHO DREAMS BIG,
I SAY: YES, YOU CAN BE ANYTHING YOU
WANT—EVEN PRESIDENT."
—HILLARY RODHAM CLINTON

· HYPATIA ·

MATHEMATICIAN AND PHILOSOPHER

Once upon a time, in the Ancient Egyptian city of Alexandria, there was a huge library. The largest library in the whole world at that point, this was a library with no books, and no paper. People wrote on papyrus (which was made from a plant), which they rolled into scrolls instead of having flat books like we have today. In this ancient library, there were thousands of scrolls, each handwritten by a scribe and carefully kept on a shelf.

In the library at Alexandria, a father and a daughter sat side by side studying scrolls together. Philosophy, math, and science were their favorite subjects.

Their names were Theon and Hypatia.

Hypatia solved equations and put forward new theories about geometry and arithmetic. She liked studying so much that soon she started to write her own books (*oops! scrolls!*). She even built an instrument, called an astrolabe, for calculating the position of the Sun, the Moon, and the stars at any given time.

Hypatia taught astronomy and her classes were always popular; students and other scholars crowded in to hear her speak. She refused to wear traditional women's clothes, and gave her lectures dressed in scholars' robes like the other teachers. Sadly, all her works were destroyed when the library burned down. But luckily, her students wrote to each other about Hypatia and her brilliant ideas, so we could also learn about this genius of Alexandria.

CA. 370–MARCH 8, 415
GREECE

ILLUSTRATION BY
RIIKKA SORMUNEN

"RESERVE YOUR RIGHT TO
THINK, FOR EVEN TO THINK
WRONGLY IS BETTER THAN NOT
TO THINK AT ALL."
— HYPATIA

IRENA SENDLEROWA

WAR HERO

In Poland, there lived a little girl called Irena who loved her father dearly. One day, a terrible epidemic of typhus broke out in their city, Warsaw. Irena's father was a brave doctor. He could have stayed away from the people who were sick, and not put himself at risk. But he chose to be with them and look after them until he, himself, fell ill with the disease.

Before he died, he said to his daughter, "Irena, if you see someone drowning, you must jump in and try to save them."

Irena cherished his words and, when Jews started to be persecuted by the Nazis, she helped Jewish families save their children.

She gave the children Christian names, and found Christian families where they could be safe. She wrote their real names and their new names on little slips of paper that she rolled up and hid in marmalade jars. Then, she buried all the jars in a friend's garden, under a big tree.

Sometimes, the smaller children would cry when Irena was taking them away. To distract the Nazi guards and cover up the noise, Irene trained a dog to bark when she told it to.

She hid children in sacks, in bags full of clothes, in boxes, even inside coffins!

In three months, she saved 2,500 children.

After the war, she dug up the marmalade jars and reunited many of the children with their families.

FEBRUARY 15, 1910–MAY 12, 2008
POLAND

"I WAS BROUGHT UP TO BELIEVE THAT IF A
PERSON WAS DROWNING, THEY MUST BE RESCUED,
REGARDLESS OF THEIR RELIGION OR NATIONALITY."
—IRENA SENDLEROWA

• ISABEL ALLENDE •

WRITER

Not long ago in Chile, there lived a passionate young girl called Isabel.

Isabel protested every time she was treated differently for being a girl. Whenever someone told her she could not do something "because she was a girl," her heart ignited with indignation.

She loved writing and was fascinated by people and their life stories, so she decided to become a journalist.

One day, she interviewed a famous Chilean poet called Pablo Neruda. "You have such a vivid imagination, you should be writing novels, not articles for a newspaper," he told her.

A few years later, Isabel got some sad news: her grandfather was dying. She was far from home, in Venezuela, and could not go back to Chile to visit him, so she started writing him a letter.

Once she started writing, she found she couldn't stop. She wrote about her family, about people who were alive and people who were dead. She wrote about a cruel dictator, about passionate love stories, a terrible earthquake, supernatural powers, and ghosts.

The letter grew so long that it turned into a novel.

The House of the Spirits became wildly successful, making Isabel one of the most famous novelists of our time. She has written twenty more books and won more than fifty literary awards.

BORN AUGUST 2, 1942
CHILE

"WRITE WHAT SHOULD NOT
BE FORGOTTEN."
—ISABEL ALLENDE

JACQUOTTE DELAHAYE

PIRATE

Once upon a time, in Haiti, there was a girl with hair as red as fire. Her name was Jacquotte.

Jacquotte's mother died while giving birth to her little brother.

Their father died not long after, and Jacquotte had to find a way to provide for herself and for her brother. So she decided to become a pirate.

Jacquotte led a gang of hundreds of pirates. Together, while at sea, they ate smoked meat, played games, pressed gunpowder in cannons, and robbed Spanish ships. She even had a secret island where she and her pirates lived!

Jacquotte had many enemies: both the government and rival buccaneers were after her. In order to escape, she decided to fake her own death and go into hiding. She gave herself a new name and dressed as a man, but her deception didn't last long. No one else had such flaming red hair! She soon returned to piracy and earned the nickname "Back from the Dead Red."

Jacquotte had a girlfriend who was a pirate too! Her name was Anne Dieu-le-Veut, and she was married and she had two children. After her husband died during a fight, she took command of their ship and joined forces with Jacquotte.

They were two of the most feared pirates of the Caribbean. Their stories became legends that both female and male pirates told each other, as they lay in their hammocks, beneath the stars, rocked by the waves, dreaming of the adventures that awaited them at dawn.

CA. 1640S–CA. 1660S

HAITI

"I COULDN'T LOVE A MAN WHO
COMMANDS ME, ANYMORE THAN
I COULD LOVE ONE WHO LETS
HIMSELF BE COMMANDED BY ME"
—JACQUOTTE DELAHAYE

JANE AUSTEN

Once upon a time, in the English countryside, there was a girl who loved books more than anything else. There was nowhere that Jane would rather be than curled up on a sofa in her father's library, with her nose in a book. She would get so engrossed in the stories that sometimes she even argued with the characters, as though they could talk back.

Jane and her seven siblings would put on plays and charades to amuse themselves and their parents. When she was still very young, she started to write her own stories, and used to read them out to her sister Cassandra to make her laugh. Jane's writing was like Jane herself: bright, inventive, witty, and sharp. To her, every detail counted: how a couple squabbled, how a man walked, what maids said to each other—these were all clues revealing people's characters. Jane jotted down everything in her notebooks, ready to use in her novels.

At that time, girls were expected to get married. But Jane didn't want to get married, so she never did.

"Oh, Lizzy! Do anything rather than marry without affection," she wrote in one of her novels.

Jane Austen came to be one of the most famous writers in the history of English literature. You can still visit the beautiful cottage in the little village where she used to sit, writing at a small desk, looking out of the window and into the flower garden.

DECEMBER 16, 1775–JULY 18, 1817
UNITED KINGDOM

ILLUSTRATION BY
SOPHIA MARTINECK

"AH! THERE IS NOTHING
LIKE STAYING AT HOME,
FOR REAL COMFORT."
—JANE AUSTEN

JANE GOODALL

PRIMATOLOGIST

Once, in England, there was a girl called Jane who loved climbing trees and reading books.

Her dream was to go to Africa and spend time with the wild animals there.

So, one day, Jane flew to Tanzania with her notebook and binoculars, determined to study real chimpanzees in their natural environment.

At first, it was hard to get close to them. The chimpanzees would run away the moment she was in sight. But Jane kept visiting the same place every day at the same time. Eventually, the chimps allowed her to get closer.

Getting closer was not enough for Jane: she wanted to become friends with them. So she started a "banana club." Whenever she visited the chimpanzees, she would share bananas with them.

At the time, little was known about chimpanzees. Some scientists used to observe them from far away, using binoculars. Others studied chimps in cages.

Jane, instead, spent hours hanging out with chimpanzees. She tried to speak to them using grunts and cries. She climbed trees and ate the same foods they ate. She discovered that chimpanzees have rituals, that they use tools, and that their language comprises at least twenty different sounds.

She even discovered that chimpanzees are not vegetarians.

Once, Jane rescued an injured chimpanzee and nursed it back to health. When she released it back into the wild, the chimpanzee turned and gave her a long, loving hug as if to say, "thanks and bye!"

BORN APRIL 3, 1934
UNITED KINGDOM

"ONLY IF WE UNDERSTAND, WILL
WE CARE. ONLY IF WE CARE,
WILL WE HELP. ONLY IF WE HELP,
SHALL ALL BE SAVED."
—JANE GOODALL

JESSICA WATSON

SAILOR

Once upon a time, there was a girl called Jessica who was afraid of water.

One summer morning, Jessica was playing with her sister and cousins by the pool. At one point, the other children lined up on the side, and got ready to jump in together holding hands.

Jessica's mom watched from the window to make sure Jessica was okay. She expected Jessica to step back from the side, but was amazed to see her daughter step forward with the others. "One…two…three…" *Splash!* All the kids landed in the water, shouting and laughing.

From that day on, Jessica started loving the water. She joined a sailing club and decided to sail around the world on her own without stopping. She painted her boat bright pink and christened her, *Ella's Pink Lady*.

She packed the boat with steak and kidney pies, potatoes, cans and cans of beans, 150 bottles of milk and lots of water, and set sail from Sydney Harbor. She was just sixteen years old.

All on her own, Jessica sailed onward. She fought against waves as tall as skyscrapers, she woke up to the most beautiful sunrises, spotted blue whales, and watched shooting stars above her boat.

Seven months later, she arrived back in Sydney. Thousands of people turned out to greet her. They rolled out a special carpet for her: bright pink, just like her boat!

BORN MAY 18, 1993
AUSTRALIA

ILLUSTRATION BY
KATHRIN HONESTA

"YOU CAN'T CHANGE
CONDITIONS—JUST THE WAY
YOU DEAL WITH THEM."
—JESSICA WATSON

· JILL TARTER ·

ASTRONOMER

Once there was a girl who wanted to become friends with the stars.

Her name was Jill.

"How can we be alone in the universe, when the sky is so big?" she used to wonder.

She couldn't stop thinking about it, so when she grew up she decided to search the skies for extraterrestrial life. She became an astronomer and director of SETI, the most important center for scientific research into the possibility of life in outer space.

For years, Jill and her team investigated hundreds of star systems, using radio telescopes located around the world. Every night she looked for signs of civilization on some distant planet.

Nobody knew—and even today nobody knows what communication systems aliens might be using. The only thing we do know is that the universe is too big for us to be its only inhabitants.

Jill especially enjoyed her solitary walks at night under the starry sky. "I'd walk to the control room to start my shift at midnight: Orion was right overhead, like an old friend," she recalls.

None of her research so far has established any scientific proof for extraterrestrial life, but she hasn't lost hope. "No one ever said there are no fish in the sea just because one glass of water came up empty," she says.

BORN JANUARY 16, 1944
UNITED STATES OF AMERICA

"SCIENTIFIC IDEAS SHINE
LIGHT INTO DARK CORNERS."
—JILL TARTER

· JINGŪ ·

EMPRESS

Once upon a time, in Japan, there lived an empress, who was expecting a child.

One day her husband, the emperor, declared war on a group of rebels. Jingū did not agree. She told him of a vision that had come to her in a dream: They should use their army to invade Korea, "a country full of marvelous things dazzling to the eye."

Jingū's husband did not take her advice: He lost the battle against the rebels and died.

While still pregnant, Jingū kept her husband's death secret, put on his clothes, and defeated the rebels herself. She then led the Japanese army across the Sea of Japan to conquer Korea, as her dream foretold.

As well as having dreams that helped her win battles, Jingū was thought to have all kinds of magical powers. People said that she controlled the tides, using two special jewels she had in her jewelry box. Others said that her son, Ōjin, remained in her womb for three whole years, giving his mother time to invade Korea and return home before giving birth.

She was probably just exceptionally talented and tough.

Jingū was a heroic warrior and never afraid to take responsibility for her actions. "If this expedition is successful, it will be due to you, my ministers; and, if not, I alone am to blame," she said.

The expedition was successful and she reigned for over seventy years.

CA. 169–269

JAPAN

"BRANDISHING OUR WEAPONS,
WE SHALL BRAVE THE TOWERING
WAVES; OUR FLEET IS READY TO
TAKE POSSESSION OF THE LAND
OF TREASURE."
—JINGŪ

· JOAN JETT ·

Joan loved rock 'n' roll. One Christmas, when she was thirteen years old, she got her first guitar.

She was ecstatic—but something was missing. Playing on her own was okay, she thought, "But if I really want to be a rock star, I need a band."

One year later, she had her band together: Sandy on drums, Cherie on vocals, Jackie played bass and Lita was the band's lead guitarist. With Joan on rhythm guitar and singing, they were…The Runaways.

They were fifteen years old, loud and proud. Onstage, Joan always wore a red leather jumpsuit, and Cherie often came on in nothing but her underwear.

"You're too young," people said.

"So what?" they shouted back.

"You're too loud," people complained.

They just played louder.

"Girls can't be punk rockers."

"Oh yeah? Just watch us!"

One of their first songs, "Cherry Bomb," was a hit.

Their second album, *Queens of Noise*, became a sensation in Japan.

It wasn't always easy, though. Back home, they toured around in a beat-up old van, traveling from town to town through the night. Sometimes people would shout at them or throw things. But the Runaways didn't care. They lived for the music; they felt raw and alive.

BORN SEPTEMBER 22, 1958
UNITED STATES OF AMERICA

"MY GUITAR IS
NOT A THING. IT
IS AN EXTENSION
OF MYSELF. IT IS
WHO I AM."
—JOAN JETT

· JULIA CHILD ·

CHEF

At six feet two inches, Julia Child was an uncommonly tall girl. When the Second World War broke out, Julia was determined to join the army. She was rejected for being too tall. The navy said she was too tall for them, too. So she became a spy.

One of her first missions was to solve a highly explosive problem. Dotted around the ocean were underwater bombs targeting German submarines. The trouble was that they kept being set off by sharks swimming too close. All the other agents were stumped—but Julia had an idea.

She started cooking.

Mixing together all sorts of disgusting ingredients, she baked cakes that smelled like dead shark when released into the water. Sharks didn't dare get close to them. You know when you spray your arms with insect repellent to keep the bugs away? She did the same, only with sharks and bombs.

After the war ended, Julia and her husband moved to France for his job. Julia's very first mouthful of French food was mind-blowing: She couldn't believe that food tasted so wonderful! No more shark repellent for her. She decided to join Le Cordon Bleu—the finest cooking school in the world— and learn everything the chefs there could teach her.

Julia became a world authority on French food and her cookbook, *Mastering the Art of French Cooking*, was a bestseller. She even had her own TV shows. *"Bon appétit,"* she said, *"*–except if you're a shark!"

AUGUST 15, 1912–AUGUST 13, 2004
UNITED STATES OF AMERICA

ILLUSTRATION BY
BARBARA DZIADOSZ

"A PARTY
WITHOUT
CAKE IS JUST
A MEETING."
—JULIA CHILD

KATE SHEPPARD

SUFFRAGETTE

There was a time when men believed women were put on earth only to serve them. They thought women should cook and clean, look after the children, and not worry about anything else. Women, so they thought, should wear "feminine clothes"—which meant long dresses with tight-laced corsets. It didn't matter that women dressed that way could hardly move or even breathe; they just had to look pretty.

Having a job was off-limits, playing sports was off-limits, and governing the country was definitely off-limits. Women were not even allowed to vote!

But Kate thought that women should have the same freedom as men: freedom to say what they thought, to vote for whom they wanted, and to wear comfortable clothes.

One day, she stood up and declared, "Women should be allowed to vote. And they should stop wearing corsets." People were shocked, outraged, and inspired by Kate's radical new ideas.

Kate and her friends gathered so many signatures on their petition that they had to paste sheets of paper together to form a long roll. They carried it into parliament and unrolled it on the floor, like a really long carpet. Imagine seventy-four ice cream trucks parked in a line—it was even longer than that! It was the longest petition ever presented. The legislators were speechless. Thanks to Kate, New Zealand became the first country in the world where women gained the right to vote.

MARCH 10, 1847–JULY 13, 1934
NEW ZEALAND

ILLUSTRATION BY MALIN ROSENQVIST

"DO NOT THINK YOUR SINGLE VOTE DOES NOT MATTER MUCH. THE RAIN THAT REFRESHES THE PARCHED GROUND IS MADE UP OF SINGLE DROPS."
—KATE SHEPPARD

· LAKSHMI BAI ·

QUEEN AND WARRIOR

Once upon a time, in the state of Jhansi, India, lived a girl who loved fighting.

She studied self-defense, archery, and swordfighting. She trained hard at weightlifting and wrestling and was a brilliant rider too. She formed her own private army with other girls who were also skilled in fighting techniques.

Lakshmi Bai married Gangadhar Rao, Maharaja of Jhansi, and became queen (Rani in Sanskrit). Lakshmi and Gangadhar had a child, but the boy died tragically young. The Maharaja never recovered from the sadness of losing a son, and died himself soon after.

At that time, the British ruled India and they wanted to rule Jhansi too. They used the death of Lakshmi's son and husband as an excuse, and ordered her to leave the palace. First Rani Lakshmi Bai tried to fight the British in court, but they refused to hear her case. So she assembled an army of 20,000 rebels, which included both women and men.

After a fierce battle, her army was overcome, but even then, Rani Lakshmi Bai did not give in. She left the city by jumping her horse down a huge wall and headed east, where she was joined by more rebels—many of whom were girls like her. Rani Lakshmi Bai led her troops back into battle, dressed as a man and on horseback.

One of the British generals remembered her as "the most dangerous of all the rebel leaders."

NOVEMBER 19, 1828–JUNE 18, 1858

INDIA

"CHARGE!"
—LAKSHMI BAI

LELLA LOMBARDI

FORMULA ONE RACER

Once there was a girl who liked to help her father deliver meats in their van. Every time they had a delivery she would jump into the driver's seat and her father would time her. Her name was Maria Grazia, but everybody called her Lella.

Lella was so good at driving that she set a new record with each delivery. Everyone in town got used to seeing the Lombardis' van driving at full speed down the hills, with salami bouncing around in the back.

When she turned eighteen, Lella used all her savings to buy a used racing car and started racing professionally. When her parents read in the newspaper that she had won the Formula 850 Championship, they weren't really surprised.

Lella didn't care that she was always the only woman in the race. She just drove as fast as she could to become a Formula One racing driver.

Her first attempt was a flop: She didn't even qualify. But the next year she found a good manager, a sponsor, and a fantastic car: white, with the Italian flag on the nose. During the Spanish Grand Prix, Lella finished sixth, becoming the first-ever female driver to score points in a Formula One race.

Despite her success, her team decided to hire another driver—a man—and Lella realized that Formula One still wasn't ready to accept women drivers.

She continued to race all her life. No other female driver has yet beaten her Formula One record.

MARCH 26, 1941–MARCH 3, 1992
ITALY

"I PREFER RACING TO
FALLING IN LOVE."
—LELLA LOMBARDI

· LOZEN ·

O nce upon a time, there was a girl who wanted to be a warrior. Her name was Lozen and she belonged to one of the Apache tribes, Native American people who originally roamed across what is now Arizona, New Mexico, and Texas.

When Lozen was still a little child, the United States Army attacked the Apache to take control of their land. Lozen saw many of her friends and relatives die in battle and, from that moment on, she vowed that she would dedicate her life to defending her tribe and her people.

"I don't want to learn women's work and I don't want to get married," she said to her brother Victorio. "I want to become a warrior."

Victorio was the leader of their tribe and taught Lozen to fight and hunt. He always wanted her by his side on the battlefield. "Lozen is my right hand," he used to say. "Strong as a man, braver than most, and cunning in strategy, Lozen is a shield to her people."

Her courage and strength were legendary. People believed she had supernatural powers that allowed her to anticipate the movements of their enemies. She became the spiritual leader of her tribe, as well as a healer. After her brother died, Lozen joined forces with the famous Apache leader Geronimo. She was eventually captured with this last group of free Apache, but her memory is still strong in the heart of all people who fight for freedom.

CA. LATE 1840s–1886
UNITED STATES OF AMERICA

ILLUSTRATION BY
MALIN ROSENQVIST

"IN THIS WORLD, THE
UNSEEN HAS POWER."
—LOZEN

MAE C. JEMISON

ASTRONAUT AND DOCTOR

Once upon a time, there was a curious girl named Mae who could not make up her mind about what she wanted to be when she grew up.

Sewing dresses for her Barbie dolls, she wanted to be a fashion designer; reading a book about space travel, she wanted to be an astronaut; fixing a broken toy, she thought maybe an engineer would be better; going to the theater, she exclaimed, "Maybe I'll become a dancer."

The world was Mae's laboratory and she had plenty of experiments she wanted to try. She studied chemical engineering, African-American studies, and medicine. She learned to speak Russian, Swahili, and Japanese. She became a doctor and volunteered in Cambodia and Sierra Leone. Then she applied to NASA to become an astronaut. Mae was selected and after one year of training, she was sent into space on board the space shuttle.

She carried out tests on the other members of the crew. Since she was not only an astronaut but also a doctor, her mission was to conduct experiments on things like weightlessness and motion sickness, which can be quite a problem when you're floating upside down in outer space.

When Mae came back to Earth, she realized that—while she had enjoyed space very much—her true passion was improving health in Africa. So she quit NASA and founded a company which uses satellites to do just that.

Mae Jemison was the first African-American woman in space.

BORN OCTOBER 17, 1956
UNITED STATES OF AMERICA

ILLUSTRATION BY
KARABO MOLETSANE

"I ALWAYS KNEW I'D
GO TO SPACE."
—MAE C. JEMISON

MALALA YOUSAFZAI

ACTIVIST

Once there was a girl who loved school. Her name was Malala.

Malala lived in a peaceful valley in Pakistan. One day, a group of armed men called the Taliban took control of the valley. They frightened people with their guns.

The Taliban forbade girls from going to school. Many people disagreed but they thought it would be safer to keep their girls at home.

Malala thought this was unfair, and wrote about it online. She loved school very much—so one day, she said on TV, "Education is power for women. The Taliban are closing girls' schools because they don't want women to be powerful."

A few days later, Malala got onto her school bus as usual. Suddenly, two Taliban men stopped the bus and shouted, "Which one of you is Malala?"

When her friends looked at her, the men fired their guns, hitting her in the head.

Malala was rushed to hospital, and she did not die. Thousands of children sent her get well cards, and she recovered faster than anyone could have imagined.

"They thought bullets would silence us, but they failed," she said. "Let us pick up our books and our pens. They are our most powerful weapons. One child, one teacher, one book, and one pen can change the world."

Malala is the youngest person ever to receive the Nobel Peace Prize.

BORN JULY 12, 1997

PAKISTAN

ILLUSTRATION BY
SARA BONDI

"WHEN THE WHOLE WORLD
IS SILENT, EVEN ONE VOICE
BECOMES POWERFUL."
—MALALA YOUSAFZAI

• MANAL AL-SHARIF •

WOMEN'S RIGHTS ACTIVIST

Once there was a girl who wanted to drive a car.

She lived in Saudi Arabia, a country where religious rules forbid women from driving.

One day she decided to break the rules.

She borrowed her brother's car and drove around the streets of her city for a while.

She posted a video on YouTube showing her at the wheel, so that as many people as possible could see what she was doing and could find the courage to do the same.

"If men can drive, why can't women?" Manal said in the video.

It was a simple question, after all. But religious authorities didn't like it.

"What if other women start to drive? They will get out of control," the authorities shouted.

So a few days later Manal was arrested and had to promise not to drive again.

Her video, in the meantime, had been watched by thousands of people. A few weeks later hundreds of brave Saudi women took the streets with their cars, defying religious authorities.

Manal was put in jail again, but she continued to speak out and to encourage women to drive and fight for their rights.

"Don't ask when this ban will be lifted. Just get out and drive."

BORN APRIL 25, 1979
SAUDI ARABIA

ILLUSTRATION BY
KATE PRIOR

"GO OUT AND DRIVE."
—MANAL AL-SHARIF

MARGARET HAMILTON

COMPUTER SCIENTIST

Once there was a girl who put a man on the Moon. Her name was Margaret and she was really good with computers.

When she was just twenty-four years old she joined NASA, the US agency that explores outer space. She took the job to support her husband and her daughter, little realizing that she would soon lead a scientific revolution that would change the world.

Margaret was an engineer and led the team who programmed the code that allowed the Apollo 11 spacecraft to land safely on the Moon's surface.

Margaret would bring her daughter Lauren to work on weekends and evenings. While four-year-old Lauren slept, her mother programmed away, creating sequences of code to be added to the Apollo's command module computer.

On July 20, 1969, just minutes before Apollo 11 touched down on the lunar surface, the computer started spitting out error messages. The entire mission was in danger. Luckily, Margaret had set up the computer to focus on the main task and ignore everything else. So instead of aborting the mission, Apollo 11 landed safely on the Moon.

The Apollo landing was hailed by the world as "one small step for man, one giant step for mankind." But it wouldn't have happened at all without the brilliant programming skills and cool-headedness of one woman: NASA engineer Margaret Hamilton.

BORN AUGUST 17, 1936
UNITED STATES OF AMERICA

"I WORKED ON ALL THE
APOLLO MANNED MISSIONS."
—MARGARET HAMILTON

MARGARET THATCHER

PRIME MINISTER

Once upon a time, in Great Britain, there was a girl who did not care about what others thought of her. She believed in doing what she thought was right. Some people liked her for being honest, others thought she was rude. Margaret just shrugged and carried on.

She studied chemistry and became a scientist, but her true passion was politics, so she tried to get elected to the British Parliament. The first time she did not make it, nor the second time, but Margaret was not one to give up.

She decided to go back to college and study law. She got married and had twins. When the next elections came, she was not even considered, because the men in her party thought that a young mother would be unsuitable for life in parliament.

Finally, a few years later, her dream came true, and Margaret was elected to Parliament. Once in Parliament, she was so successful, she became leader of the Conservative Party, and then Prime Minister—the first female Prime Minister in British history.

When she took free milk away from primary school children, the people disliked her. When she won the war against Argentina in the Falkland Islands, people admired her strength and determination.

Margaret liked to work hard and was immensely practical. Sometimes, people tried to pressure her into making decisions she did not agree with, but she never bowed. That's why she became known as The Iron Lady.

OCTOBER 13, 1925–APRIL 8, 2013
UNITED KINGDOM

"YOU MAY HAVE TO
FIGHT A BATTLE MORE
THAN ONCE TO WIN IT."
—MARGARET THATCHER

MARGHERITA HACK

ASTROPHYSICIST

Once upon a time, in the *Via delle Cento Stelle* (Street of a Hundred Stars) in Florence, a little girl was born. Her name was Margherita and she would grow up to become an incredible astrophysicist (a scientist who studies the properties of stars and planets).

While she was studying physics, she became increasingly interested in stars: "We are part of the evolution of the universe," she said. "From the calcium in our bones to the iron in our blood, we're entirely made of elements created in the heart of stars. We really are 'children of the stars'."

Margherita's favorite place was the Arcetri Observatory. High on a hill above Florence, she would scan the skies through a huge telescope, her mind full of questions: How do galaxies evolve? How far are the stars from each other? What can we learn from starlight?

Margherita traveled the world, giving lectures and inspiring others to study the stars. Back in Florence, she became Italy's first woman director of an astronomical observatory.

Margherita said that some of her best friends were stars. Their names were Eta Boo, Tauri, Zeta Her, Omega Tau and 55 Cygni. She even had an asteroid named after her!

For Margherita, being a scientist meant basing your knowledge of the natural world on facts, observations, and experiments, and being passionately curious about the mystery of life.

JUNE 12, 1922–JUNE 29, 2013
ITALY

"THE STARS ARE NOT VERY
DIFFERENT FROM US: THEY
ARE BORN, THEY GROW
OLD, THEY DIE."
—MARGHERITA HACK

ILLUSTRATION BY
CRISTINA SPANÒ

· MARIA CALLAS ·

OPERA SINGER

Maria was a clumsy and unpopular girl.

She was sure that her mother loved her sister more because her sister was slimmer, prettier, and more popular than her.

One day, Maria's mother discovered that her little daughter had an amazing voice. She encouraged Maria to sing in order to earn money for their family.

Maria's mother tried to enroll her in the National Conservatory in Athens, but Maria was rejected because she had never had any formal training. So her mother sent her to a private teacher.

When her teacher first heard her sing, she was speechless. It was the most amazing voice she had ever heard. Not only did Maria master all the most difficult arias in a matter of a few months, her singing style went straight to the heart.

Maria applied to the National Conservatory again and this time she was accepted.

One night, she made her debut on the stage of the most prestigious opera house in the world: La Scala in Milan. When she sang, the audience hung on to every note and every word as her voice carried them away to a place full of passion, rage, joy, and love. At the end, they jumped to their feet, clapping and shouting, and showered the stage with roses.

Maria came to be known simply as La Divina, the divine one—the most famous soprano ever.

DECEMBER 2, 1923–SEPTEMBER 16, 1977

GREECE

"I WILL ALWAYS BE
AS DIFFICULT AS
NECESSARY TO ACHIEVE
THE BEST."
—MARIA CALLAS

MARIA MONTESSORI

PHYSICIAN AND EDUCATOR

Once upon a time, there was a teacher who worked with disabled children. Her name was Maria and she was also a doctor.

Instead of applying old teaching methods, Maria watched children to see how they learned. In her school, children were not forced to do what the teacher told them to do. They could move about freely and choose whatever activity they loved the most.

Maria's innovative techniques proved to be very effective with disabled children, so she decided to open a school for all children and apply the same teaching methods. She called her school the Children's House.

For the Children's House, Maria invented child-sized furniture: small, light, chairs that children could move around easily, low shelves, so they could reach things without needing a grown-up.

Maria also invented toys that encouraged children to discover the world in very practical and independent ways. In her classes, children discovered how to button and unbutton their shirts, how to carry a glass of water without spilling it, how to lay the table by themselves.

"Children should be taught to be self-sufficient," she said. "If they know how to tie their shoes and how to dress themselves, they will feel the happiness that comes from independence."

Maria Montessori's method is applied in thousands of schools and it helps children all over the world grow strong and free.

AUGUST 31, 1870–MAY 6, 1952
ITALY

ILLUSTRATION BY
CRISTINA SPANÒ

"NEVER HELP A CHILD
WITH A TASK AT WHICH
SHE FEELS SHE CAN
SUCCEED."
—MARIA MONTESSORI

· MARIA REICHE ·

ARCHAEOLOGIST

I n a small house in a Peruvian desert, there lived an adventurous German mathematician called Maria Reiche.

Etched into the dry desert rocks were hundreds of lines. No one knew what they were for, or why they were there, or even how old they were.

These mysterious lines, called *Nazca lines*, became Maria's passion. She flew planes and helicopters to map the lines and–when there were no planes to fly–she just climbed the tallest ladder she could find to observe the lines from above. Some lines had been covered by dust so she used brooms to clean them. She used so many brooms that some people thought she was a witch!

As she studied the lines, she discovered something incredible. Those were not just random scratches: They were enormous drawings—made by the people who lived there thousands of years ago. There was a hummingbird! Intertwined hands! Flowers! A gigantic spider! All sorts of geometrical shapes!

Why would these ancient people create drawings that could only be seen from the sky? What were they? It was a mystery she was determined to solve.

She found that the lines corresponded to the constellations in the night sky. "It's like a giant map of the heavens," she said.

When Maria moved from Germany to Peru, she wasn't looking for giant mysterious drawings. But when she found them, she knew she would spend the rest of her life trying to figure them out. She became known as "The Lady of the Lines."

MAY 15, 1903–JUNE 8, 1998
GERMANY

"WHEN I FIRST CAME TO PERU
BY SEA, THE SHIP PASSED
THROUGH THE CENTER OF FOUR
CONSECUTIVE RAINBOWS: FOUR
ARCS, ONE INSIDE THE OTHER."
—MARIA REICHE

MARIA SIBYLLA MERIAN

NATURALIST

Maria was a little girl who loved art. Every day, she would gather flowers to paint. Sometimes, she found caterpillars on the flowers and made paintings of how they changed, day by day, into beautiful butterflies.

At that time, people believed that butterflies magically sprouted out of mud. Maria knew better, but no one believed her.

Years passed and Maria became a great watercolor artist. She wrote about her discoveries, but at the time scientists only took books in Latin seriously, and Maria's was in German.

One day, Maria and her daughter decided to move to a new city: Amsterdam. There, Maria found display cases filled with exotic insects collected from South America.

Maria thought, "If I could study these insects in their natural habitat, I could write a book that people would notice."

She sold her paintings and set sail to South America. In the rainforests of Suriname, Maria and her daughter climbed tall jungle trees to study the insects high up. Maria wrote her new book in Latin and this time, it was a huge success. Everybody learned that butterflies and moths come from caterpillars, not mud! The process is called *metamorphosis* (from the Latin word meaning *to change shape*). Today, we know that many animals metamorphosize: frogs, moths, beetles, crabs…and all thanks to the work of Maria Sibylla Merian!

APRIL 2, 1647–JANUARY 13, 1717
GERMANY

ILLUSTRATION BY
AMANDA HALL

"IN MY YOUTH, I SPENT MY
TIME INVESTIGATING INSECTS."
—MARIA SIBYLLA MERIAN

• MARIE CURIE •

SCIENTIST

Once, in Poland, there was a secret school. People called it the Floating University.

The government at that time was very strict about what people could and couldn't study. Girls were not allowed to go to college at all.

Marie and her sister were students at the secret school, but they were tired of hiding.

One day, they heard that in Paris there was a university called the Sorbonne, which accepted girls, so they decided to move to France.

Marie was fascinated by metals and magnets. She found out that some minerals were radioactive. They gave off powerful rays and glowed in the dark. To analyze these minerals' properties, Marie would set them on fire, melt them, filter them, and stay up all night to watch them glow. Radiation is used to treat many diseases, but it is also very dangerous. Just imagine that, after all these years, Marie's notebooks and instruments are still radioactive. If you want to look at them, you have to wear protective clothing and gloves.

Marie's husband, Pierre, was so intrigued by her research that he decided to drop his work on crystals to join her. Together they discovered two new radioactive elements: polonium and radium.

Marie Curie won two Nobel Prizes for her work and she could have made a lot of money from her discoveries. She chose, instead, to make her research available to anyone for free.

NOVEMBER 7, 1867–JULY 4, 1934
POLAND

ILLUSTRATION BY
CLAUDIA CARIERI

"NOTHING IN LIFE
IS TO BE FEARED.
IT IS ONLY TO BE
UNDERSTOOD."
—MARIE CURIE

· MARY ANNING ·

PALEONTOLOGIST

In a tiny, cramped house on the south coast of England, there lived a girl called Mary. Her house was so close to the sea that sometimes the storms would flood it.

The winds and storms that swept along the coast often revealed fossils in the cliffs along the shoreline. These are the remains of prehistoric plants or animals that died a long time ago.

Mary could not go to school because her family was too poor, but she taught herself to read and write. She studied geology to learn more about rocks, and anatomy to learn more about the skeletons of the prehistoric animals she found.

One day, she saw a strange shape jutting out of a rock. Mary took out her special little hammer and carefully chipped away at the rock. Bit by bit, she uncovered a thirty-foot-long skeleton. It had a long beak, but it wasn't a bird. Rows of sharp teeth, but it wasn't a shark. Flippers, but it wasn't a fish. And a long thin tail! It was the first ever discovery of that kind of dinosaur fossil, and she named it *ichthyosaur*, meaning *fish-lizard*.

At the time, people believed that the Earth was only a few thousand years old. Mary's fossils helped prove that there had been life on our planet for hundreds of millions of years.

Scientists from all over the world came to see Mary, the self-taught scientist who loved walking by the sea.

MAY 21, 1799–MARCH 9, 1847
UNITED KINGDOM

"MY NAME IS WELL KNOWN THROUGHOUT EUROPE."
—MARY ANNING

MARY EDWARDS WALKER

SURGEON

Once upon a time, there was a girl called Mary who wore whatever clothes she wanted: boots, pants, ties, shirts.

At that time, girls were expected to wear tightly laced corsets and layers of petticoats under their skirts. It was hard to move or even breathe in clothes like that. But unlike all her friends' parents, Mary's mom and dad thought that everyone, including girls, should wear whatever they liked. Her father, a self-taught country doctor, thought that all of his children would be happier and healthier in comfortable trousers and shirts, especially in the hot, humid summers. Mary was happy about that—she much prefered boys' clothes anyway.

Mary, her sisters, and her brother were encouraged by their father to study.

Mary wanted to be a doctor, so she attended medical school and graduated as one of the first female doctors in the United States.

Mary married a fellow doctor and she wore trousers and a coat for their wedding, because she liked that outfit more than a traditional wedding dress.

When the Civil War broke out, she stepped forward to serve in the Union Army.

A few times, Mary was arrested for dressing in men's clothes. But to Mary, those were just clothes—she just wore what she wanted.

She saved many lives during the Civil War and was awarded a Congressional Medal of Honor once it had ended. She wore the medal her whole life, on the collar of her coat, next to her tie.

NOVEMBER 26, 1832–FEBRUARY 21, 1919
UNITED STATES OF AMERICA

ILLUSTRATION BY
ELIZABETH BADDELEY

"LET THE GENERATIONS KNOW
THAT WOMEN IN UNIFORM ALSO
GUARANTEED THEIR FREEDOM."
—MARY EDWARDS WALKER

MARY KOM

BOXER

O nce upon a time, in India, there was a little girl called Mary. Mary's family was very poor and struggled to put food on the table. Mary wanted to help her family live a better life, so she decided to become a boxer.

One day, she boldly walked up to the coach in a boxing gym. "Will you train me?" she asked. "You're too tiny," he said. "Go away."

But when the coach finished for the day, he found her still waiting for him by the gate. "I want to do this. Put me in the ring," she said to him.

Reluctantly, he took her on and she started training hard. She started competing, and won many fights. But she hadn't told her parents—she didn't want to worry them.

One day, her dad read about her in a newspaper. "Is this you?" he asked, worried. "Yes," said Mary, proudly. "What if you get hurt?" her mother asked. "We don't have the money for doctors!"

"I will work hard, and save as much as I can. Don't worry," Mary replied.

She slept in hostels, ate vegetables and rice because could not afford meat, skipped breakfast because she only had money for lunch and dinner, and she became a champion.

Her parents watched her fights on TV. Mary won medal after medal. She even won a medal at the Olympics! She made her village proud, and was able to provide for her family, just like she had dreamed when she was a child.

BORN MARCH 1, 1983

INDIA

ILLUSTRATION BY
PRIYA KURIYAN

"WITHOUT BOXING, I CAN'T
LIVE. I LOVE BOXING."
—MARY KOM

MATILDE MONTOYA

DOCTOR

Once upon a time, in Mexico, there lived a woman called Soledad who had a little girl whose name was Matilde. Soledad soon realized that her daughter was exceptionally bright. She could read and write by the time she was four, and was ready for high school by the time she was eleven.

When she turned sixteen, Matilde started training as a midwife. But she had bigger dreams: she wanted to be a doctor.

When she joined the National School of Medicine, she was the only female student. Lots of people told her that a woman could never be a doctor, but she had her mom and many friends on her side.

At the end of her first year, the university tried to expel Matilde.

Matilde wrote a letter to the President of Mexico asking for his help. He wrote to the university telling them to stop being so unfair to her. She finished her course, but then the university stopped her from going in for her final exam.

Again, she wrote to the president and again he stepped in. This time, he passed a law that allowed all women to study medicine and become doctors.

The president himself traveled all the way to the university to see her take her final exam. It was a historic moment.

The next day, newspapers across the country celebrated the story of 'la Señorita Matilde Montoya', Mexico's first ever female doctor.

MARCH 14, 1859–JANUARY 26, 1939
MEXICO

ILLUSTRATION BY
CRISTINA PORTOLANO

"I AM A DOCTOR."
—MATILDE MONTOYA

MAUD STEVENS WAGNER

TATTOO ARTIST

Once there was a girl who liked tattoos. Her name was Maud and she was a circus performer.

Maud was a great aerialist and contortionist. People would come to see her fly through in the air every night.

One day, she met a man called Gus Wagner who had his body completely covered with tattoos: monkeys, butterflies, lions, horses, snakes, trees, women—anything you can think of!

"I am a walking, talking work of art!" he used to say.

Maud liked his tattoos so much that she agreed to go out with him, if he gave her a tattoo.

Gus first made one tattoo on her body, then another, and another…until Maud's body was also completely covered with tattoos.

Maud was a quick learner and soon began working as a tattooist for other circus performers and for the public, all while she continued to perform as an acrobat on the circus and carnival circuit.

At the time, tattoos were unusual and people would flock to the circus to gawk at scantily clad women, their bare skin covered with ink.

Maud and Gus worked so well together that they became inseparable. They eventually got married and spread the art of tattooing beyond circus sideshows and across the country.

Maud is the first known female tattoo artist in the United States.

FEBRUARY, 1877–JANUARY 30, 1961
UNITED STATES OF AMERICA

ILLUSTRATION BY
GIULIA FLAMINI

"GIVE ME A TATTOO."
—MAUD STEVENS WAGNER

MAYA ANGELOU

WRITER

Once there was a little girl who didn't speak for five years. She thought her words could hurt people and promised herself to never make a peep again. Her name was Maya.

People thought Maya was crazy, but in fact she was simply scared. "I know you will speak again one day," her grandmother kept telling her. "You will find your voice," her beloved brother said.

Maya listened to them and began to memorize everything she heard or read: poems, songs, short tales, random conversations. "It was like putting a CD on. If I wanted to, I'd run through my memory and think, that's the one I want to hear," she later recalled.

She became so good at memorizing words, that when she started to write it was like music was flowing from her pen. She wrote about her childhood, growing up in a town where African-Americans were treated badly for the color of their skin.

Her writing became the voice of the Civil Rights Movement and all the people fighting for the rights of African-Americans. She constantly reminded us that everyone, black or white, male or female, has equal rights.

In addition to her many books, Maya was so talented that she also wrote songs, plays, and movies, and acted onstage and onscreen. "See me now, black, female, American and Southern," she once said to a group of black students. "See me now and see yourselves. What can't you do?"

APRIL 4, 1928–MAY 28, 2014
UNITED STATES OF AMERICA

"MY MISSION IN LIFE IS NOT MERELY TO
SURVIVE, BUT TO THRIVE; AND TO DO SO
WITH SOME PASSION, SOME COMPASSION,
SOME HUMOR, AND SOME STYLE."
—MAYA ANGELOU

MAYA GABEIRA

SURFER

Once upon a time, there was a girl who liked big waves. Not the ones that you splash around in at the seaside. Not even the ones that you see from the pier. She liked super-mega-gigantic monster waves and wanted to become the Superwoman of Surfing.

"Not again, Maya," her mom would wail, as her daughter headed off to the beach. "You're always wet and cold, and everyone else surfing is a guy!" But Maya didn't care: Surfing was her passion. "And as for the guys, well, they'd better get used to me!" she said.

She started traveling the world in search of the biggest waves possible: Australia, Hawaii, Portugal, Brazil. Maya would jump on a plane and go anywhere to catch the next big one. Once, in South Africa, she rode a wave fourteen meters high—the highest ever for a female surfer. She won every major competition and became the highest-paid big wave surfer in the world.

But one day, while she was surfing in Portugal, a wave caught her by surprise. The wall of water crashed over her, dragging her underwater. She broke bones and almost drowned before her partner rescued her and gave her CPR. After such a scary incident, most people would have been afraid to go back in the water and maybe thought about a career change.

Not Maya.

As soon as she healed Maya went right back to the same beach in Portugal. "I love it," she says. "The surf around here is epic."

BORN APRIL 10, 1987
BRAZIL

"I RAN A LOT, SURFED A
LOT, AND WORKED A LOT."
—MAYA GABEIRA

• MELBA LISTON •

TROMBONIST

Once there was a small girl who wanted to play the trombone. Her name was Melba.

When Melba was seven, a traveling music store came to town. She saw a bright, shiny brass instrument, and Melba just knew she had to have one. "That?" exclaimed her mother. "For a little bitty girl? Why, it's almost as tall as you are!" But Melba insisted. "It's the most beautiful thing I've ever seen."

Melba started to play her trombone every day. She tried to go to music lessons, but she didn't get along with her teacher. "I'll learn on my own. I'll just play it by ear," she said. It was hard, but she loved the bold, brassy sound the instrument made. Within a year, she was good enough to play solo trombone on the local radio station.

When she was still a teenager, Melba toured the United States with a band led by trumpet player Gerald Wilson. A few years later, she was hired to accompany Billie Holiday—one of the greatest jazz singers of all time— on a tour in the South.

The tour wasn't as successful as they expected, so when Melba returned home she decided to give up playing. But her passion was too strong: She soon returned to writing and playing music. She even came out with a solo album, *Melba Liston and her 'Bones* (short for *trombones*). She also arranged music for other musicians, weaving rhythms, harmonies, and melodies into gorgeous songs for all the jazz greats of the twentieth century.

JANUARY 13, 1926–APRIL 23, 1999
UNITED STATES OF AMERICA

"LOOK HOW SHINY IT IS!"
—MELBA LISTON

· MICHAELA DEPRINCE ·

BALLERINA

Once, a girl called Michaela lost her parents during a terrible war. Michaela had *vitiligo*, a skin condition which caused white spots on her neck and chest. Because of how she looked, the people at the orphanage called her "the devil's daughter." Little Michaela was lonely and scared—but so was a girl called Mia.

When Michaela was afraid, Mia would sing her a song. When Mia could not sleep, Michaela would tell her a bedtime story. They became best friends.

One day, the wind blew a magazine to the gates of the orphanage. On the cover was a picture of a beautiful lady in a sparkly dress, her toes pointed. "She's a ballerina," Michaela's teacher told her.

"She looks so happy," four-year-old Michaela thought. "I want to be like her."

Soon afterward, she was taken on a long journey. She and Mia got separated. To stop herself from being scared, Michaela started to dream.

She dreamed that she and Mia had a mom and that she was a ballerina.

At the end of the journey, a lady came up to her saying that she wanted to adopt not only Michaela but Mia too!

All of Michaela's dreams were coming true. So where was her tutu? She started searching around. "What are you looking for?" asked her new mom. Michaela showed her the magazine.

"You can be a ballerina too," her mom said, smiling.

Michaela devoted herself to ballet classes and is now a ballerina with the Dutch National Ballet.

BORN JANUARY 6, 1995
SIERRA LEONE

ILLUSTRATION BY
DEBORA GUIDI

"NEVER BE AFRAID TO BE A POPPY
IN A FIELD OF DAFFODILS."
—MICHAELA DEPRINCE

• MICHELLE OBAMA •

LAWYER AND FIRST LADY

Once upon a time, there was a girl who was always afraid.

Her name was Michelle Robinson and she lived in a one-bedroom apartment in Chicago with her family.

"Maybe I'm not smart enough. Maybe I'm not good enough," she worried. And her mother would say, "If it can be done, you can do it."

"Anything is possible," said her dad.

Michelle worked hard. Sometimes, teachers told her she should not aim too high because her grades were not that good. Some people said she would never achieve something big, because "she was just a black girl from the South Side of Chicago."

But Michelle chose to listen to her parents. "Anything is possible," she thought. So she graduated from Harvard and became a lawyer at a big firm. One day, her boss asked her to mentor a young lawyer. His name was Barack Hussein Obama.

They fell in love and got married a few years later.

One day, Barack told her he wanted to become President of the United States. At first, she thought he was crazy, but then she remembered: "If it can be done, you can do it." So she quit her job and helped him on his campaign.

Barack won the elections (twice!) and Michelle became the first African-American First Lady of the United States. "No one is born smart. You become smart through hard work," is her motto.

BORN JANUARY 17, 1964
UNITED STATES OF AMERICA

"ALWAYS STAY TRUE TO YOURSELF AND
NEVER LET WHAT SOMEBODY ELSE SAYS
DISTRACT YOU FROM YOUR GOALS."
—MICHELLE OBAMA

MILLO CASTRO ZALDARRIAGA

DRUMMER

Once there was a small girl who dreamed of playing the drums. She lived on an island full of music, colors, and delicious papayas. Her name was Millo.

Everyone on the island knew that only boys were allowed to play drums. "Go home," they would shout at Millo. "This is not for girls."

They didn't know that Millo's passion for drums was stronger than a coconut crab.

During the day, she would listen to all the sounds around her. The sound of palm trees dancing in the wind; the sound of hummingbirds flapping their wings; the sound of jumping into a puddle with both feet—SPLASH!

At night, she would sit on the beach and listen to the sound of the sea.

"Why can't I also be a drummer?" she would ask to the breaking waves.

One day, Millo convinced her father to take her to a music lesson. Timbales, conga, bongos. . . . She could play anything! The teacher was so impressed that started to give Millo lessons every day.

"I will play in a real band," Millo kept saying.

When her sister Cuchito put together Anacaona, Cuba's first ever all-girl dance band, ten-year-old Millo joined as drummer. They soon had everyone dancing.

Millo became a world-famous musician. She even played at an American president's birthday party when she was only fifteen.

BORN CA. 1922
CUBA

ILLUSTRATION BY
SARAH WILKINS

"GIRLS CAN DRUM!"
—MILLO CASTRO ZALDARRIAGA

THE MIRABAL SISTERS

ACTIVISTS

When a cruel dictator named Raphael Trujillo took the power in the Dominican Republic, four sisters started to fight for freedom. They were the Mirabal sisters: Minerva, Patria, Maria Teresa, and Dedé. People called them *Las Mariposas*, the butterflies.

They distributed pamphlets and organized a movement to protest Trujillo and restore democracy in their country. Trujillo didn't like it.

In his worldview, girls like the Mirabal sisters were a good company for parties. They were supposed to compliment him, receive flowers and gifts, smile and say "thank you." They were not supposed to raise their voices, to disagree, and even try to overturn his regime! The Butterflies' fierce independence scared him, so he tried several different strategies to silence them.

He put them in jail, he barred them from practicing law, he imprisoned Minerva and her mother in a hotel room . . . he even tried to seduce Minerva! But Minerva said no. She was not up for sale. She didn't care about becoming the girlfriend of a powerful tyrant. She only cared about freedom for her country.

The sisters' courage inspired Dominicans and gave them strength to oppose Trujillo's regime. Eventually, he was taken down.

On the 137-foot obelisk that Trujillo had erected to celebrate his power, today there's a mural celebrating the Mirabal sisters, four butterflies who defied a tyrant.

PATRIA, FEBRUARY 27, 1924–NOVEMBER 25, 1960; MINERVA, MARCH 12, 1926–NOVEMBER 25, 1960; MARIA TERESA, OCTOBER 15, 1935–NOVEMBER 25, 1960; DEDE, MARCH 1, 1925–FEBRUARY 1, 2014
DOMINICAN REPUBLIC

"WE CANNOT ALLOW OUR
CHILDREN TO GROW UP
IN THIS CORRUPT AND
TYRANNICAL REGIME."
—PATRIA MIRABAL

ILLUSTRATION BY
RITA PETRUCCIOLI

• MIRIAM MAKEBA •

ACTIVIST AND SINGER

Once upon a time, the people of South Africa were treated very differently, according to the color of their skin.

It was illegal for black and white people to spend time with each other or to fall in love and have children.

This cruel system was called *apartheid*.

Into this world came a little girl who loved to sing. Every Sunday, Miriam went to church with her mother. She was so desperate to sing in the choir that she used to sneak in the back whenever they were rehearsing.

When Miriam grew up, she recorded more than a hundred songs with her all-girl band, the Skylarks.

She sang about life in South Africa: what brought her joy, what made her sad, what got her angry. She sang about dancing and about apartheid.

The people loved her songs, especially one called "Pata Pata" which was her biggest hit. But the government did not like the anti-apartheid message of Miriam's music. They wanted to silence her voice of protest. When Miriam left the country on tour, they took away her passport and wouldn't let her back into the country.

Miriam toured the world and she became a symbol of the proud African fight for freedom and justice. People started calling her "Mama Africa."

After thirty-one years she was allowed back home. Shortly afterward, apartheid was finally crushed.

MARCH 4, 1932–NOVEMBER 9, 2008
SOUTH AFRICA

"EVERYBODY STARTS TO
MOVE AS SOON AS 'PATA
PATA' STARTS TO PLAY."
—MIRIAM MAKEBA

MISTY COPELAND

BALLERINA

I t was a beautiful night when Misty stepped onstage before a hushed audience to dance the leading role in a ballet called *The Firebird*.

Misty was the only African-American in one of the world's most famous dance companies, and this was the first time she had danced as a prima ballerina.

As the curtain rose, her arms moved gracefully as the wings of a bird, she turned pirouettes and soared across the stage in long, beautiful jumps. The audience was transfixed.

When final curtain fell, she revealed something no one could have imagined. She had hurt her leg, and had been in great pain throughout the whole performance. She had six fractures in her left shin and needed surgery.

It seemed impossibly cruel that the very night she had achieved her dream, she was told she might never dance again.

For Misty, that was unacceptable: She loved dance too much. Dance had found Misty when she was thirteen years old, living in a motel with her mom and her five siblings. Dance had found her when she had never thought she could earn a living by doing something she was passionate about.

So she went through the surgery, through therapy, and worked harder than ever to be fit enough to dance again with the American Ballet Theatre.

She danced in *Swan Lake*, a true black swan, stronger and more elegant than ever.

BORN SEPTEMBER 10, 1982
UNITED STATES OF AMERICA

"DANCE FOUND ME."
—MISTY COPELAND

ILLUSTRATION BY
PING ZHU

NANCY WAKE

SPY

Once there was a girl who became a secret agent.

When she was just sixteen years old, she traveled by herself from Australia to England and convinced a newspaper to hire her. When the Second World War broke out, she joined the French Resistance (the *Maquis*) in their fight against the Nazis.

After escaping to England, Nancy parachuted back into France so she could help train and organize resistance fighters and rescue British pilots who had been shot down over France. She got them fake identity papers and then ferried them across the mountains to Spain, so they could get back to Britain safely.

She outwitted the German secret police (the *Gestapo*) at every turn and was soon top of their Most Wanted list. They nicknamed her *The White Mouse*, because she seemed impossible to catch!

Nancy was also a great soldier. She was a great shot and never lost her nerve. When her unit suffered a surprise attack by the Germans, she took command of a section whose leader had been killed and, with exceptional coolness, organized a retreat with no further losses.

When the war ended and France was finally liberated, Nancy was awarded the George Medal by the British. The French gave her three Croix de Guerre medals and the Médaille de la Résistance. They later made her a Knight of the Legion of Honor—their highest award. The Americans awarded her the Medal of Freedom.

AUGUST 30, 1912–AUGUST 7, 2011
NEW ZEALAND

ILLUSTRATION BY
MONICA GARWOOD

"FOR GOODNESS SAKE, DID
THE ALLIES PARACHUTE ME
INTO FRANCE TO FRY EGGS
AND BACON FOR THE MEN?"
—NANCY WAKE

NANNY OF THE MAROONS

QUEEN

Once upon a time, in Jamaica, there lived an escaped slave with royal African ancestors. Her name was Queen Nanny, and she was the leader of a group of escaped slaves called the Maroons.

At the time, Jamaica was occupied by the British. They enslaved Africans and deported them to Jamaica to work on sugarcane plantations. But Queen Nanny wanted freedom for herself and for her people, so she escaped, freed many other slaves, and led them into the mountains where they built a village called Nanny Town.

The only way to Nanny Town was along a narrow path through the jungle. Queen Nanny taught the Maroons to cover themselves with leaves and branches to blend in with the jungle.

As British soldiers walked through the forest in single file, they had no idea they were surrounded. But at the sound of a signal, the "trees" around them suddenly leaped to life and attacked.

Nanny Town had one problem, though. Its inhabitants were hungry.

One night, weak with hunger and worried for her people, Queen Nanny fell asleep. She dreamed of one of her ancestors who told her: "Don't give up. Food is at hand."

When she woke up, she found pumpkin seeds in her pockets. She planted them on the hillside and soon her tribe had plenty of food.

From then on, the hill near Nanny Town was called Pumpkin Hill.

CA. 1686–1733

JAMAICA

ILLUSTRATION BY
CAMILLA PERKINS

"I AM FREE NOW."
—NANNY OF THE MAROONS

NELLIE BLY

In a village in Pennsylvania, there was a girl who always dressed in pink. Her name was Nellie.

When her father died, the family fell on hard times. She went out looking for a job to help her mom make ends meet.

One day, Nellie read an article in a local newspaper. It was about "What Girls are Good For." In the article, girls who worked were described as "monsters," because the author believed that a woman's place was in the home. Furious, Nellie wrote a passionate letter to the editor.

Impressed by her writing style, the editor offered her a job as a reporter.

Nellie proved soon to be a brave investigative journalist. She moved to New York and joined the *New York World,* a newspaper run by a famous man called Joseph Pulitzer. Once, she pretended to be mentally ill and got herself checked into a mental institution to expose how badly the patients were treated. She was fearless, clever, and compassionate.

The newspaper set her a challenge. Jules Verne had written a popular novel called *Around the World in Eighty Days*: Could she do it in less time? It took Nellie just a few hours to pack a small bag and set sail from New York in a steamer. Traveling by ship, rail, and even donkey, she set herself a grueling pace. People placed bets on whether she would succeed or fail. Finally, 72 days, 6 hours, and 11 minutes later, she arrived back in New York. She had made it!

MAY 5, 1864–JANUARY 27, 1922
UNITED STATES OF AMERICA

"I HAVE NEVER WRITTEN A WORD THAT DID NOT COME FROM MY HEART. I NEVER SHALL."
—NELLIE BLY

THE NEW

NELLIE BLY

BEST REPORTER IN THE U.S.

· NETTIE STEVENS ·

GENETICIST

Once upon a time, there was a teacher called Nettie Stevens who decided she wanted to become a scientist. She saved as much money as she could and—when she was thirty-five—she moved to California to attend Stanford University.

While she was at the university she became obsessed with finding out why it was that boys become boys and girls become girls. The answer, she was sure, lay in studying cells.

Humanity had been concerned with this question for almost two thousand years. Scientists and philosophers had invented all sorts of theories to explain it: some said it depended from the body temperature of the dad, some other said it was about nutrition . . . basically, no one had a clue.

In order to crack this mystery once and for all, Nettie started studying mealworms.

After studying their cells for hours under a microscope, she made an important discovery: Female larvae had twenty large chromosomes, while male larvae had only nineteen large chromosomes plus one smaller one.

"Bingo!" shouted Nettie, eyes still glued to the microscope.

A scientist called Edmund Wilson made a similar discovery at about the same time, but he failed to realize quite how important this was. Wilson thought that gender was also affected by the environment, but Nettie said, "Nope. It's all down to the chromosomes." And she was right.

JULY 7, 1861–MAY 4, 1912
UNITED STATES OF AMERICA

ILLUSTRATION BY
BARBARA DZIADOSZ

"I'LL WELCOME QUESTIONS FROM
STUDENTS SO LONG AS I KEEP MY
ENTHUSIASM FOR BIOLOGY; AND THAT, I
HOPE, WILL BE AS LONG AS I LIVE."
—NETTIE STEVENS

· NINA SIMONE ·

SINGER

Nina was a gifted, proud girl. When her mom was at church, Nina, unnoticed, climbed up the organ bench and learned to play "God Be with You Till We Meet Again." She was three years old then.

When she was five years old, her mother's employer offered to pay for piano lessons and Nina started training to become a classical pianist.

She was committed, hardworking, and hugely talented.

At twelve, she gave her first concert. Her parents were sitting in the front row, but they were forced to move to the back of the hall to make room for some white people who came in. Nina refused to start playing until her parents were seated back at the front.

Nina poured her passion and pride into her music and she could not stand racism. She wanted black people to be proud, to be free, to embrace their talents and their passions, free of judgement.

That's why she wrote songs like "Brown Baby," or "Young, Gifted and Black." Nina Simone knew how racism hurt black people, and she wanted them to find strength in her songs. "The worst thing about that kind of prejudice" she said "is that while you feel hurt and angry and all the rest of it, it feeds your self-doubt. You start thinking, perhaps I am not good enough."

Nina decided to cultivate her talent, rather than her fear, and eventually, she became one of the most famous jazz singers in the world.

FEBRUARY 21, 1933–APRIL 21, 2003
UNITED STATES OF AMERICA

ILLUSTRATION BY
T.S. ABE

"I TELL YOU WHAT FREEDOM
IS TO ME: NO FEAR."
—NINA SIMONE

POLICARPA SALAVARRIETA

SPY

Once upon a time, in Bogotá, Colombia, there was a seamstress who was also a spy. Her real name was secret, but most people knew her as Policarpa Salavarrieta.

When she was a child, Policarpa's godmother taught her how to sew. Little did she know that one day, her sewing skills would help bring about a revolution in her country.

At the time, Colombia was ruled by faraway Spain. Many people, called *royalists*, were proud that they had a Spanish king. Others were revolutionaries like Policarpa: they wanted Colombia to be free.

The royalists were always on the lookout for revolutionaries. Policarpa had to keep changing her name to avoid being captured.

Policarpa worked as a seamstress in the houses of royalists. While she was altering clothes for the ladies, she gathered information about royalist plans, which she would pass on to her revolutionary friends.

One day, a messenger carrying information provided by Policarpa was caught, and her secret identity was uncovered. She was arrested and told that her life would be spared only if she gave them the names of her friends.

She looked them straight in the eye and said, "I'm a young woman, and you can't scare me."

Policarpa still inspires women and men from Colombia and from all over the world to fight for freedom and justice without fear.

JANUARY 26, 1795–NOVEMBER 14, 1817
COLOMBIA

"I HAVE MORE
THAN ENOUGH
COURAGE."
—POLICARPA
SALAVARRIETA

RITA LEVI MONTALCINI

SCIENTIST

When Rita's nanny died of cancer, she decided to become a doctor.

She was particularly fascinated by neurons (the stuff our brain is made of). So after graduation, Rita worked with an extraordinary professor named Giuseppe Levi and with a group of outstanding fellow scientists from her class.

They were in the middle of some very important research when a cruel dictator passed a law saying that Jewish people were not allowed to work at the university.

She escaped to Belgium with her professor, who was also Jewish. But when the Nazis invaded Belgium, she had to escape again and returned to Italy.

It is hard to work as a scientist when you have to hide all the time and you have no access to a lab, but Rita did not give up.

She turned her bedroom into a small research lab. She sharpened sewing needles to create surgical instruments. She placed a small operating table in front of her bed where she dissected chickens, and studied cells under a microscope.

When her city was bombed, Rita escaped again, then again. From hideout to hideout, no matter how difficult, wherever she went, she kept on working.

For her work in the area of neurobiology, she was awarded the Nobel Prize for Medicine—which made her the third person from her medical school class to win a Nobel Prize!

APRIL 22, 1909–DECEMBER 30, 2012
ITALY

"ABOVE ALL, DON'T FEAR
DIFFICULT MOMENTS. THE
BEST COMES FROM THEM."
—RITA LEVI MONTALCINI

ROSA PARKS

ACTIVIST

Once upon a time, Montgomery, Alabama, was a segregated city. Black people and white people went to different schools, prayed in different churches, shopped in different stores, rode different elevators, and drank from different drinking fountains. Everyone rode the same buses, but they had to sit in different areas: white people up front, black people at the back. Rosa Parks grew up in this black-and-white world.

It was hard for black people and many were angry and sad because of segregation, but if they protested they were thrown in jail.

One day, forty-two-year-old Rosa was sitting in the back of a bus on her way home from work. It was crowded and there were not enough seats in the front section (the one reserved for whites), so the driver told Rosa to give up her seat so a white person could sit down.

Rosa said no.

She spent the night in jail, but this one brave act showed people that it was possible to say no to injustice.

Rosa's friends declared a boycott. They asked every single black person not to use any of the buses in the city until the law was changed. The word spread fast and wide. The boycott lasted for 381 days. It ended when bus segregation was declared unconstitutional by the U.S. Supreme Court.

It took ten years for segregation to be banned in any other state, but it happened, finally, thanks to Rosa's first, brave "No."

FEBRUARY 4, 1913–OCTOBER 24, 2005
UNITED STATES OF AMERICA

ILLUSTRATION BY
SALLY NIXON

"I WOULD LIKE TO BE REMEMBERED
AS A PERSON WHO WANTED TO BE
FREE...SO OTHER PEOPLE WOULD
BE ALSO FREE."
—ROSA PARKS

RUTH BADER GINSBURG

SUPREME COURT JUSTICE

Once upon a time, there was a girl who dreamed of becoming a great lawyer. "A lady lawyer?" people would mock her. "Don't be ridiculous! Lawyers and judges are always men."

Ruth looked around her and saw that they were right. "But there's no reason why that shouldn't change," she thought to herself.

She applied to Harvard Law School and became one of its brightest students.

Her husband, Marty, was also a student at Harvard. "Your wife should be home baking cookies and looking after the baby," people used to say. But Marty didn't listen. Ruth was a terrible cook! And besides, he loved taking care of their daughter, and was proud of his brilliant wife.

Ruth was passionate about women's rights and argued six landmark cases on gender equality before the United States Supreme Court. Then she became the second female Supreme Court Justice in the country's history.

There are nine justices on the Supreme Court. "If I'm asked, when will there be enough women on the Supreme Court, I say, 'When there are nine.' People are shocked—but there've been nine men, like forever, and nobody's ever raised their eyebrows at that."

Even in her eighties, Ruth does twenty push-ups every day and has become a style icon, thanks to the extravagant collars she wears in court with her judge's robes.

BORN MARCH 15, 1933
UNITED STATES OF AMERICA

"I DISSENT."
—RUTH BADER GINSBURG

RUTH HARKNESS

EXPLORER

A long time ago, zoos didn't know much about how to care for the animals they acquired. It was rare for an exotic animal to survive the trip to America. Visitors were used to seeing dead, stuffed animals. It was hard to feel sympathy for a stuffed animal.

So when Ruth's husband decided to bring back a live panda from China, it was a big deal. Sadly, just a few months after arriving in China, her husband died.

Ruth was a fashion designer in New York City and knew little about China. But she missed her husband and she loved adventures. So she thought, "I'll finish what Bill started. I'll go to China and bring back a live panda."

In China, Ruth hiked through the thickest forests, climbed her way up to ancient monasteries, followed rivers by day and made fire by night.

One night, she heard a sound. Ruth followed the noise into the forest and found a baby panda in a tree hollow. She took it in her arms and didn't know what to do. She gave the panda milk. When she was back in the city, she bought a fur coat, so the baby panda would feel better when she held it.

She called the panda Su Lin and she brought the panda all the way from China to the Chicago Zoo. Tens of thousands of people saw how cute Su Lin was, and learned that all wild animals deserve respect and love.

SEPTEMBER 21, 1900–JULY 20, 1947
UNITED STATES OF AMERICA

ILLUSTRATION BY
CLAUDIA CARIERI

"I DON'T KNOW WHETHER IT WILL
BE HUMANLY POSSIBLE TO GET A
PANDA OR NOT, BUT I FEEL THAT
IF IT IS, I WILL."
—RUTH HARKNESS

· SEONDEOK OF SILLA ·

QUEEN

Once upon a time, in Silla, one of the three kingdoms of Korea, there was a very clever fourteen-year-old girl who became queen. A nobleman called Lord Bidam didn't like this at all, and led an uprising against Seondeok with the slogan "Girls can't be Kings!" He saw a falling star, and said that was a sign that her reign would fall soon.

But Seondeok flew a burning kite and told the people that her star was back in the sky.

That was not the first time that Seondeok amazed everyone with a clever stunt. When she was a child, her father the king had been given a packet of poppy seeds and a painting of poppies by the Emperor of China. "These will be beautiful flowers," she said, looking at the illustration on the packet, "it's just a shame they won't have a sweet scent."

"How do you know that?" her father asked.

"If they were scented, there would have been bees or butterflies in the picture."

When the flowers bloomed, it turned out she was right: They were indeed odorless.

The young queen sent scholars and students to China to learn Chinese languages and customs, forging strong ties of friendship between their countries.

Seondeok was the first queen of Silla, after twenty-six kings.

CA. 606–FEBRUARY 17, 647

KOREA

ILLUSTRATION BY
KIKI LJUNG

"WHAT IS HARDER THAN
GAINING PEOPLE'S
TRUST IS HAVING TO
ABANDON THEM."
—SEONDEOK
OF SILLA

SERENA AND VENUS WILLIAMS

TENNIS PLAYERS

Once upon a time, there was a man named Raul. He ran a taco stand that stood on a street corner in the city of Compton.

Every day, Raul saw a man and his two daughters walk past his stand and head to the tennis court nearby. The man's name was Richard Williams and his daughters were Venus and Serena. Every day, Richard took a basket of tennis balls to the court and showed his two daughters how to play.

Serena was just four years old at the time. She was so small that when she sat on the bench, her feet didn't touch the ground. She was often the youngest player in the tournaments her father entered her in—but that didn't stop her from winning.

In Compton there were gangs who would sometimes cause trouble, but when they saw Venus and Serena playing tennis, they were inspired by their passion and determination. They stood by the court in awe, and made sure no one disturbed the sisters.

Venus and Serena trained hard, giving their all to tennis. By the time they were teenagers, they were so strong that their father declared they were on their way to becoming the best tennis players in the world.

And that's exactly what happened! Both sisters have been ranked number 1 in the world.

They continue to make Raul, their father, and the whole city of Compton very proud.

SERENA, BORN SEPTEMBER 26, 1981; VENUS, BORN JUNE 17, 1980
UNITED STATES OF AMERICA

"I'M REALLY EXCITING. I
SMILE A LOT, I WIN A LOT,
AND I'M REALLY SEXY."
—SERENA WILLIAMS

SIMONE BILES

GYMNAST

Once there was a girl who could fly. Her name was Simone Biles. Simone Biles was a gymnast, the greatest in American history. When Simone took to the mat, people couldn't take their eyes off her. She was so fast, so strong, so flexible, so agile! She flew through the air with such grace and speed, twisting and turning, and landing perfectly each time.

Simone started gymnastics when she was just six years old. By the time she was eighteen, she had already won so many medals, that when she traveled to Rio for the Olympics everyone expected her to win not one, but five medals.

One day, a journalist asked her, "How do you deal with that kind of pressure?"

"I try not to think about it. Right now, my goal is to be more consistent on the uneven bars."

"What about the goal of winning a gold medal?"

"A medal can't be a goal," Simone replied, smiling. "It's like my mom always says: 'If doing your best means you come out on top, that's awesome. If it means that you finish fourth, that's awesome too."

Simone's mom adopted her when Simone was three. She taught Simone that staying humble and doing your best is the only way to live a meaningful life and to inspire everyone around you.

At the Olympics in Rio, Simone won five medals—four of them gold!

BORN MARCH 14, 1997
UNITED STATES OF AMERICA

"I WAS BUILT THIS WAY
FOR A REASON, SO I'M
GOING TO USE IT."
—SIMONE BILES

SONITA ALIZADEH

RAPPER

When Sonita was ten years old, her parents told her, "We have to sell you into marriage." They started buying her nice clothes and taking more care of her than they had done before.

Sonita did not know exactly what all this meant, but she knew she did not want to get married: She wanted to study, to write, and to sing songs. She told her mother so. Her mother said to her, "We need the money to buy a bride for your older brother. There is no choice. We must sell you."

At the last moment, the marriage arrangements fell through. War broke out in Afghanistan, where the family lived, and Sonita and her brother were sent away to live in a refugee camp in Iran. Sonita went to a school nearby and she started writing down her songs.

When Sonita was sixteen years old, her mom came to visit her. She told Sonita that she had to go back to Afghanistan because they had found another husband who wanted to buy her. Again, Sonita said no. Sonita loved her mom, but she did not want to get married. She wanted to be a rapper.

She wrote a hard-hitting song called "Brides for Sale" and uploaded it on YouTube. The video went viral and Sonita became famous. She won a scholarship to study music in America. "In my country, a good girl should be silent," says Sonita, "but I want to share the words that are in my heart."

BORN 1996
AFGHANISTAN

"I AM TIRED OF THE SILENCE."
—SONITA ALIZADEH

ILLUSTRATION BY
SAMIDHA GUNJAL

· SYLVIA EARLE ·

MARINE BIOLOGIST

Once upon a time, there was a young scientist who loved to dive at night, when the ocean is dark, and you can't tell if the fish are asleep or awake.

"At night," she said, "you see lots of fish you don't see in the daytime."

Her name was Sylvia.

Sylvia led a team of aquanauts: she and her team lived underwater for weeks, dived out of all kinds of underwater vehicles, and studied life in the ocean like no one before.

One night, Sylvia wore a special suit. White and gray, and as big as a space suit, it had a huge, domed helmet with four round windows to see out of. Six miles offshore, she dived deeper than anyone had ever been without a rescue tether. Down where the dark is blacker than the starless night, with only the feeble light of an underwater lamp, she put her foot on the ocean floor, just as the first man, in a similar costume but miles above her head, had put his footprint on the surface of the Moon.

"Without the ocean," she explained, "there would be no life on earth. No humans, no animals, no oxygen, no plants. If we don't know the ocean, we can't love it."

Sylvia has studied hidden currents, discovered underwater plants, and waved to deep-sea fish. "We must take care of the oceans," she says. "Will you join me in a mission to protect the Earth's blue heart?"

BORN AUGUST 30, 1935
UNITED STATES OF AMERICA

"I'VE HAD THE JOY OF SPENDING THOUSANDS OF HOURS UNDER THE SEA. I WISH I COULD TAKE PEOPLE ALONG TO SEE WHAT I SEE AND TO KNOW WHAT I KNOW."
—SYLVIA EARLE

ILLUSTRATION BY GERALDINE SY

TAMARA DE LEMPICKA

PAINTER

In an elegant house in Saint Petersburg, Russia, a painter came to paint a portrait of a twelve-year-old girl named Tamara.

Tamara did not like his work and thought she could do much better.

A few years later, at the opera with her aunt, Tamara spotted a man in the crowd. She knew instantly that this was the man she would marry—and so she did. His name was Tadeusz.

There was a revolution in Russia and Tadeusz was thrown in jail. Tamara managed to get him released, and organized their escape to Paris.

Paris was the center of the art world at that time, and it was here that Tamara realized her childhood dream of becoming an artist. She became famous. Celebrities lined up to be painted by Tamara.

When the Second World War broke out, Tamara moved to America. Slowly, her bold and striking style fell out of fashion. When a show of hers got bad reviews, she lost her temper and swore never to exhibit again.

Tamara moved to Mexico where she lived in a beautiful house until her death at the age of eighty-two, with her daughter Kizette by her side.

She asked that her ashes be scattered over the volcano of Popocatepetl: a fitting end for an artistic genius with an explosive personality.

Today, her paintings are worth millions of dollars. Tamara would be proud to know that the singer Madonna is one of her biggest fans.

MAY 16, 1898–MARCH 18, 1980
POLAND

"I LIVE LIFE IN THE
MARGINS OF SOCIETY,
AND THE RULES OF
NORMAL SOCIETY DON'T
APPLY TO THOSE WHO
LIVE ON THE FRINGE."
TAMARA DE LEMPICKA

VIRGINIA WOOLF

WRITER

Once upon a time, a little girl living in London created a newspaper about her family. Her name was Virginia.

Virginia was witty, cultured, and very sensitive. Whenever something bad happened, she would feel incredibly sad for weeks. When she was happy, she was the happiest kid on earth.

"I lived in intensity," Virginia wrote in her diary.

Virginia suffered from an illness known as depression. These mood swings affected her throughout her life. But whatever her mood, Virginia was always writing. She kept a diary, she wrote poems, she wrote novels, she wrote reviews. Writing was a way for her to see her own feelings more clearly and by doing so, shed light on everyone's feelings.

There was someone whom Virginia loved as much as writing: her husband, Leonard.

Virginia and Leonard were incredibly happy together and loved each other dearly, but sometimes Virginia's depression made it hard for her to feel joy. At that time, there was no effective treatment for depression, and many people did not believe it was real.

Today, depression can be treated. But whether you are happy or sad or somewhere in between, it is always a great idea to record your moods in a diary. You may become a writing genius like Virginia, and help other people understand their feelings and live lives full of dreams.

JANUARY 25, 1882–MARCH 28, 1941
UNITED KINGDOM

"I AM ROOTED, BUT I FLOW."
—VIRGINIA WOOLF

WANG ZHENYI

ASTRONOMER

Once upon a time, in China, there was a young girl who liked to study all sorts of things. She loved math, science, geography, medicine, and writing poetry. She was also great at horse riding, archery, and martial arts. Her name was Wang.

Wang traveled widely and was curious about everything but above all, she loved astronomy. She spent hours studying the planets, the Sun, the stars, and the Moon.

At that time, people thought that a lunar eclipse was a sign that the gods were angry. Wang knew this couldn't be true and decided to prove it with an experiment. She put a round table—the Earth—in a garden pavilion, and from the ceiling she hung a lamp—the Sun. Off to one side, she placed a big round mirror—the Moon.

Then she started to move these objects exactly as they move in the sky until the Sun, Earth, and Moon stood in a line, with the Earth in the middle. "There you go! A lunar eclipse happens every time the Moon passes directly through the Earth's shadow."

Wang also understood the importance of making math and science accessible for common people, so she got rid of all the aristocratic language and wrote a paper explaining the force of gravity.

Her reputation spread far and wide. In her poems, she often wrote about the importance of equality between men and women.

1768–1797

CHINA

ILLUSTRATION BY
ANA GALVAÑ

"DAUGHTERS CAN ALSO BE HEROIC."
—WANG ZHENYI

WANGARI MAATHAI

ACTIVIST

Once upon a time, in Kenya, there was a woman called Wangari. When lakes started to dry up and streams started to disappear near her village, Wangari knew she had to do something. She called a meeting with some of the other women.

"The government cut down trees to make room for farms, but now we need to walk for miles to collect firewood," one said.

"Let's bring the trees back," exclaimed Wangari.

"How many?" they asked.

"A few million should do it," she replied.

"A few million? Are you crazy? No nursery is big enough to grow that many!"

"We're not buying them from a nursery. We'll grow them ourselves at home."

So Wangari and her friends gathered seeds from the forest and planted them in cans. They watered and looked after them until the plants were about a foot tall. Then, they planted the saplings in their backyards.

It started with a few women. But, just like a tree sprouting from a tiny seed, the idea spread and grew into a widespread movement.

The Green Belt Movement expanded beyond Kenyan borders. Forty million trees were planted and Wangari Maathai was awarded the Nobel Peace Prize for her work. She celebrated by planting a tree.

APRIL 1, 1940–SEPTEMBER 25, 2011
KENYA

"THE TIME IS NOW."
—WANGARI MAATHAI

WILMA RUDOLPH

ATHLETE

Long ago, before the vaccine for polio was discovered, children were not protected against this terrible disease. Wilma was a little child when she contracted polio and was left with a paralyzed leg.

"I'm not sure she's ever going to walk again," the doctor said.

"You will walk again, honey. I promise," whispered Wilma's mom.

Every week, her mom took Wilma to the city for treatment. Every day, her twenty-one brothers and sisters took turns massaging her weak leg. Wilma had to use braces to walk, and the mean kids in her neighborhood would make fun of her. Sometimes, when her parents were not home, she tried to walk without braces. It was hard, but Wilma slowly got stronger.

By the time she was nine, her mom's promise came true. Wilma could walk by herself! She even started playing basketball.

She loved jumping and running, so she did not think twice when her coach asked if she wanted to join the track team.

Wilma competed in twenty races, and won every one of them.

"I don't know why I run so fast," she said. "I just run."

Wilma became the fastest woman in the world, bringing great joy to her family and to her country. She broke three world records at the 1960 Olympics.

Wilma always said that the key to winning was knowing how to lose: "Nobody wins all the time. If you can pick up after a crushing defeat, and go on to win again, you are going to be a champion someday."

JUNE 23, 1940–NOVEMBER 12, 1994
UNITED STATES OF AMERICA

"MY DOCTORS TOLD ME
I WOULD NEVER WALK
AGAIN. MY MOTHER TOLD
ME I WOULD. I BELIEVED
MY MOTHER."
—WILMA RUDOLPH

· XIAN ZHANG ·

ORCHESTRA CONDUCTOR

Once upon a time, there was a country where pianos were forbidden. Pianos were not sold in stores and they were not played in concerts. They simply were nowhere to be found.

One day, a man had a smart idea: He bought all the required pieces and built a piano himself. He did not build it to play it, though. He built it for his four-year-old daughter, Zhang.

Zhang loved playing so much that she became a piano teacher and trained singers at the Central Opera House in Beijing. She was happy and thought that she would be a piano teacher and a pianist for her whole life.

One night, after the final rehearsal of *The Marriage of Figaro* (a beautiful opera), the orchestra conductor called Zhang and she told her, without further explanation, "Tomorrow, you are going to conduct."

"Thank you," she squeaked. She was terrified!

The following day, she called the orchestra for an extra rehearsal. She was tiny, only twenty years old. When she stepped onto the podium, some of the musicians laughed at her.

She did not blink. She did not smile. She just raised her baton and waited.

After ten minutes, the whole orchestra was following her with respect.

"My life changed overnight," she said.

Today, Zhang is one of the most important orchestra conductors in the world.

BORN 1973
CHINA

"WHEN GIRLS SEE OTHER
WOMEN DOING THIS JOB,
THEY WILL FEEL THAT THEY
CAN DO IT, TOO."
—XIAN ZHANG

YAA ASANTEWAA

One upon a time, in a land rich with gold, lived a strong queen who ruled over the Asante kingdom. Her name was Yaa.

Her people believed in the magical powers of a golden stool which was so sacred that even the king and queen were not allowed to touch it. It was said that the heart and soul of the Asante people—past, present and future—was contained in this golden throne.

One day, a governor-general appointed by the British announced that the British Empire would be taking over the Asante lands. "We also demand your Golden Stool to sit upon. Bring it here immediately."

The Asante leaders were shocked and insulted—but their enemy was powerful. One by one, they urged surrender.

Not Yaa Asantewaa. She stood up.

"If you, the men of Ashanti, will not go forward, then we, the women, will. We will fight the white men."

Yaa led an army of 5,000 into battle against the well-equipped British soldiers. After a fierce fight, Yaa's army was defeated. She herself was captured and deported to the Seychelles Islands.

She never saw her beloved land again, but her country continued to be inspired by her bravery. A few years after her death, the Asante Empire regained its independence. To this day, Yaa Asantewaa's people still sing songs about their beloved queen and her proud, fighting spirit.

CA. 1840–OCTOBER 17, 1921

GHANA

ILLUSTRATION BY
NOA SNIR

"IF YOU, THE MEN OF
ASHANTI, WILL NOT
GO FORWARD, THEN
WE WILL. WE, THE
WOMEN, WILL."
—YAA ASANTEWAA

YOKO ONO

ARTIST

Once upon a time, a little girl called Yoko lived in a beautiful house in Tokyo. When war broke out, her house was bombed. Yoko and her family fled for their lives. Suddenly, she and her brother had no toys, no beds, no snacks, no clothes. They had to beg for food. Other children taunted them because they had once been rich, and now they were the poorest of the poor.

When she grew up, Yoko became a performance artist. You didn't just look at Yoko's art, you were part of it. For example, she asked people to cut up her clothes while she was still wearing them.

One day, a musician called John Lennon went to visit one of Yoko's exhibitions. He found her art beautiful and became a fan.

John and Yoko started writing letters to each other and they eventually fell madly in love. They recorded songs together, created photography projects and even movies.

At the time, America was at war with Vietnam. Yoko knew how bad war could be and she wanted to help the peace movement. Many protesters held "sit-ins" but, being Yoko, she wanted to do something different. Instead of a sit-in, John and Yoko had a "bed-in" where they stayed in bed for a week surrounded by television cameras and journalists.

They even recorded a song to sum up their simple, strong message: "Give peace a chance."

BORN FEBRUARY 18, 1933
JAPAN

YUSRA MARDINI

SWIMMER

Once, in Damascus, Syria, there was a swimmer called Yusra.

Every day, she and her sister trained with their dad at the local swimming pool. Syria was at war, and one day a bomb was dropped on the swimming pool. Luckily, Yusra was not there at the time.

Shortly afterward, her house was destroyed by another bomb. It was another narrow escape. All of a sudden, Yusra and her family had nothing left and nowhere to live, so they decided to flee the country.

Yusra had heard that Germany was a good place for swimmers. The journey was long and getting there would be hard, but that did not put Yusra off.

She and her sister joined a group of other refugees for a month long journey across several countries and then on board a rubber dinghy to the island of Lesbos.

The boat was only meant for six or seven people. There were twenty crammed aboard. Suddenly, the motor broke down. "We can't die at sea," Yusra thought. "We are swimmers!" And so she jumped into the water with her sister and another boy.

They kicked and swam and dragged and pushed the boat for more than three hours, until they finally reached the shore.

When they reached Germany, the first question Yusra asked was, "Where can I find a swimming club?"

Not only did she find one, in 2016 she was part of the first refugee team ever to compete in the Olympics.

BORN MARCH 5, 1998
SYRIA

ILLUSTRATION BY
JESSICA COOPER

"I WANT ALL REFUGEES
TO BE PROUD OF ME."
—YUSRA MARDINI

ZAHA HADID

ARCHITECT

Whan Zaha turned ten, she decided that she wanted to be an architect. Zaha was a very determined girl, and she grew up to be one of the greatest architects of our time. She became known as the Queen of the Curve because the buildings she designed had so many bold, sweeping lines.

One day, she boarded a plane at the airport. The pilot explained that there would be a short delay before they could take off. Zaha was outraged and insisted that they put her on a different flight immediately. It was impossible, the crew said: The baggage was already on board. But Zaha insisted—and she got her way. She usually did.

That was just who she was.

Zaha liked to cross boundaries, to do things everyone else thought were impossible. That is how she created the kind of buildings no one else could even imagine.

She designed fire stations, museums, villas, cultural centers, an aquatic center, and much more.

Zaha forged her own pathway. She was never afraid of being different. One of her mentors said she was like "a planet in her own inimitable orbit."

She always knew what she wanted and did not rest until she got it. Some say that is the key to achieving anything big in life. Zaha was the first woman to receive the Royal Institute of British Architects Gold Medal.

OCTOBER 31, 1950–MARCH 31, 2016
IRAQ

ILLUSTRATION BY
NOA SNIR

"I ALWAYS THOUGHT I WAS
POWERFUL, SINCE I WAS A KID."
—ZAHA HADID

WRITE YOUR STORY

Once upon a time, _____

_____

_____

_____

_____

_____

_____

_____

_____

_____

_____

_____

_____

_____

_____

_____

_____

_____

_____

_____

_____

_____

_____

_____

_____

_____

• DRAW YOUR PORTRAIT •

REBELS' HALF OF FAME

Here's to the rebel girls and boys who were early believers in *Good Night Stories for Rebel Girls* on Kickstarter. They come from all over the world and they're going to change the world.

NIGISTE ABEBE

PIPER ABRAMS

HAIFA AND LEEN AL SAUD

SHAHA F. AND WADHA N. AL-THANI

NEDA ALA'I-CHANGUIT

RAFFAELLA AND MADDALENA ALBERTI

MADELEINE ALEXIS

WILLOW ALLISON

LEIA ALMEIDA

VIOLET AMACK

BROOKLYN ANDERSON

SOFIA ANDREWS

ANDHIRA JS ANGGARA

GRACE ANKROM

OLIVIA ANN

SYLVIE APPLE

ALEJANDRA PIEDRA ARCOS

CAMILA ARNOLD

CAROLINA ARRIGONI

EVANGELINE ASIMAKOPOULOS

PHOEBE ATKINS

AUDREY B. AVERA

AZRAEL

MISCHA BAHAT

KIERA BAIRD

EMERY AND NYLAH BAKER

MOLLY AND SCARLET BARFIELD

EVA BARKER

ISABELLA BARRY

PIPPA BARTON

CRISTINA BATTAGLIO

SOFIA BATTEGODA

JENNIFER BEEDON

EMMA BEKIER

TAYLOR BEKIER

VIVIENNE BELA

MADELINE BENKO

EMMA BIGKNIFE

PIA BIRDIE

HANNAH BIRKETT

ALEXIS BLACK

KATIE BLICKENSTAFF

ADA MARYJO AND ROSE MARIE BODNAR

GABRIELLA MARIE BONNECARRERE WHITE

RIPLEY TATE BORROMEO

MEGAN BOWEN

LILA BOYCE

MARLEY BOYCE

MOLLY MARIE AND MAKENNA DIANE BOYCE

JOY AND GRACE BRADBURY

MAGNOLIA BRADY

EVA AND AUGUST BRANCATO

CORA AND IVY BRAND

TALA K AND KAIA J BROADWELL

AUDREY AND ALEXANDRA BROWN

SCARLETT BRUNER

MARLOWE MARGUERITE BÜCKER

KATIE BUMBLEBEE

VIVIAN AND STACY BURCH

CLARA BURNETTE

MIA A. BURYKINA

ZOE BUTTERWORTH

CASSIA GLADYS CADAN-PEMAN

GIGI GARITA AND LUNA BEECHER
CALDERÓN

FINLEY AND MANDIE CAMPBELL

SCARLETT AND CHARLI CARR

KAITLYN CARR

EMILIE CASEY

LUCIENNE CASTILLO

KYLEE CAUSER

OLIVIA ANNA CAVALLO STEELE

NEVEYA CERNA-LOMBERA ESTRADA

ELLE CHANDLER

JOSIE CHARCON

LYN CHEAH

ANNA MARY CHENG

ELINOR CHIAM

LEELA CHOUDHURI

MILA CHOW

BEATRICE CICCHELLI

COCO COHEN

ABIGAIL COLE

EMILY ROBBINS COLEY

SOPHIA CONDON

EMILY COOLEY

ALLISON COOPER

STELLA AND MATILDE CORRAINI

GIORGIA CORSINI

LOGAN COSTELLO

EMILY CLARE AND CHARLOTTE GIULIA
COSTELLO

CAMILLE AND ARIANE COUTURE

ISABEL CRACKNELL

ROSE CREED

SOPHIA AND MAYA CRISTOFORETTI

NATALIE SOPHIA AND CHLOE SABRINA CRUZ

GABRIELA CUNHA

EVIE CUNNINGHAM

ADA CUNNINGHAM

EVENING CZEGLEDY

ANTONIA AND INDIANA D'EGIDIO

KYLIE DAVIS

ELLA-ROSE DAVIS

BRENNA DAVISON

ELIZABETH DEEDS

ILARIA AND ARIANNA DESANDRÉ

ROSALIE DEVIDO

ALISZA DEVIR

PAOLA AND ANTONIO DI CUIA

EMILIA DIAZ

NEVAEH DONAZIA

HADLEY DRAPER LEVENDUSKY

HATTIE AND MINA DUDEN

SELMA JOY EAST

ALDEN ECKMAN

EUGENIO AND GREGORIO

SOPHIA EFSTATHIADIS

JULIA EGBERT

AILLEA ROSE ELKINS

ANNA ERAZO

RAMONA ERICKSON

MADELINE "MADDIE" ESSNER

ELENA ESTRADA-LOMBERA

SCOUT FAULL

LILLIAN FERGUSON

AURELIA FERGUSON

HEIDI AND ANOUSHKA FIELD

PAIGE AND MADELYN FINGERHUT

MARILENA AND TERESA FIORE

MARGARET AND KATHERINE FLEMING

VIDA FLORES SMOCK

LILY AND CIARA (KIKI) FLYNN

SABINE FOKKEMA

MIA AND KARSON FORCHELLI

HANNAH FOSS

SARA BON AND HANNAH LEE FOWLER

SYLVIE FRY

MOLLY CHARLOTTE FUCHS

KATARINA GAJGER

OLIVIA GALLAGHER

TAYLOR GALLIMORE

ANN GANNETT BETHELL

MADELINE AND LUCY GERRAND

MAREN AND EDEN GILBERT TYMKOW

FABULOUS GIRL

CAMILLA GOULD

SYAH GOUTHRO

EMMA GRANT

ISLA GREEN

CARA AND ROWAN GREEN

VICTORIA GREENDYK

MARIAH GRIBBLE

SAGE GRIDER

SUSIE GROOMES

EMMA, LUCY, AND FINLEY GROSS

CLAUDIA GRUNER

PAZ GUELFI-SALAZAR

VIOLA GUERRINI

IRIS GUZMAN

ABIGAIL HANNAH

ANNA-CÉLINE PAOLA HAPPSA

ALANNA HARBOUR

EVELYN AND LYDIA HARE

GWYNETH AND PIPER HARTLEY

ABIGAIL AND CHRISTA HAYBURN

SOFIA HAYNES

EVIE AND DANYA HERMAN

MACY HEWS

CLARE HILDICK KLEIN

AUREA BONITA HILGENBERG

RUBY GRACE HIME

AVA HOEGH-GULDBERG

JANE HOLLEY-MIERS

FARAH HOUSE

ARYANNA HOYEM

SASKIA AND PALOMA HULT

JORJA HUNG

HAYLIE AND HARPER HUNPHREYS

NORA IGLESIAS POZA

DEEN M. INGLEY

AZALAYAH IRIGOYEN

MIRIAM ISACKOV

JADI AND ALEXANDRA

MAYA JAFFE

FILIPPA JAKOBSSON

HADDIE JANE

ELEANOR HILARY AND CAROLINE KARRIE

JANULEWICZ LLOYD

JEMMA JOYCE TOBER

MARLEE AND BECCA K. ICKOWICZ

SLOANE AND MILLIE KAULENTIS

JESSICA AND SAMANTHA KELLOGG

MALENA KLEFFMAN

BRONWYN KMIECIK

CHARLOTTE KNICKERBOCKER

VIOLET KNOBLOCK

RACHEL BELLA KOLB

GABBY AND COCO KOLSKY

MILA KONAR

DARWYN AND LEVVEN KOVNER

OLIVIA KRAFT

SHAYNA AND LAYLA KRAFT

ZORA KRAFT

LUCY AND LOLA KRAMER

MORGAN AND CLAIRE KREMER

CLARA LUISE KUHLMANN

VIVIENNE LAURIE-DICKSON

JULIA LEGENDRE

BOWIE LEGGIERE-SMITH

ARIANNA LEONZIO

DARCY LESTER

ARABELLA AND KRISTEN LEVINE

EMILIA LEVINSEN

SOFIA LEVITAN

GWYNETH LEYS

ERICA A. AND SHELBY N. LIED

IRENE LINDBERG

AUDREY LIU-SHEIRBON

SYDNEY LOERKE

ROXANNE LONDON

SIENA AND EMERY LONG

GIULIA LORENZONI

BRIE LOVE

LILY KATHRYN LOWE

ELLAMARIE MACARI-MITCHELL

NATALIA MACIAS

ALISON AND CAROLINE MACINNES

MACKENZIE AND MACKAYLA

IESHA LUCILE MAE

AISLINN MANUS

LUCIA MARGHERITA

MOXIE MARQUIS

LEONOR AND LAURA MARUJO TRINDADE

CARYS MATHEWS

EVELYN AND TEAGAN MCCORMICK

VIOLET MCDONALD

JOSEPHINE, AYLIN AND SYLVIA MCILVAINE

ALIZE AND VIANNE MCILWRAITH

ANNABELLE MCLAUGHLIN

MAGGIE MCLOMAN

FIONA MCMILLEN

SOPHIA MECHAM

RYLIE MECHAM

MAILI MEEHAN

AVA MILLER

MORGAN MILLER

NOA MILLER

KATHERINE MILLER

PHOEBE MOELLENBERG

ALEXANDRA LV MOGER

LUBA AND SABRINA MIRZA MORIKI

FRIDA MORTENSEN

SARAH MOSCOWITZ

VIOLET J. MOURAS

MABEL MUDD

GEORGIANA MURRAY

NOOR NASHASHIBI

BEATRICE NECCHI

SYDNEY NICHOLS

ELLEN NIELSEN

DYLAN AND MARGAUX NOISETTE

VALENTINA NUILA

SUMMER O'DONOVAN

KSENIA O'NEIL

RIN O'ROURKE

ZELDA OAKS

OLIVIA SKYE OCAMPO

EMMA OLBERDING

CLAIRE ORRIS

ELEANORA OSSMAN

CHAEYOUNG AND CHAEWON OUM

KHAAI OWENS

MAJA AND MILA OZUT

POPPY OLIVIA PACE

OLIVIA PANTLE

SIMRIN MILA AND SIANA JAYLA PATEL

ANNAMARIA AND ELIO PAVONE

TINLEY PEHRSON

OAKLEY PEHRSON

SIENA PERRY

SCARLETT PETERS

ALEXANDRA AND GABRIELLE PETTIT

FEI PHOON

SUNNY AND HARA PICKETT

MACYN ROSE PINARD

BRESLYN, ARROT, AND BRAXON PLESH
STOCK-BRATINA

MADISYN, MALLORY, AND RAPHAEL PLUN-
KETT

FRANCES SOPHIA POE

ELSA PORRATA

ALEXANDRA FRANCES RENNIE

ANNA AND FILIPPO RENZI

AVA RIBEIRO

MIKAYLA RICE

ZOE RIVERA

ARIA AND ALANA ROBINSON

CLEO ROBINSON

SOFIA, BEATRICE, AND EDOARDO ROCHIRA

SOPHIE ROMEO

ELLA ROMO

LUCY ROTE

SOFÍA RUÍZ-MURPHY

SILVIA SABINI

ELIZABETH SAFFER

VIOLA SALA

MANUELA SALES STEELE

ESMIE SALINAS

KAYLA SAMPLE

KYRA SAMPLE

MIA AND IMANI SANDHU

SOFIA SANNA

KENDRA SAWYER

LUCY SCHAPIRO

NORAH ELOISE SCHMIT

BELLA SCHONFELD

ELISENDA SCHULTZ

MOLLY SCOTT

KYLIE AND KAITLYN SCOTT

NATALIE SER TYNG WANG

AMAYA AND KAVYA SETH

CRISTINA AND EVELYN SILVA

SHAI SIMPSON

ELLA AUSTEN AND KAILANI MEI SKOREPA

PHOEBE SMITH

ARLENE SMITH

OLIVIA-LOUISE SMITH

SARA SNOOK

EVERLY SNOW

GENEVIEVE AND EMERY SNYDER

SELIA SOLORZANO

AURORA SOOSAAR

AVA STANIEWICZ

RHYAN STANTON

BROOKE STARCHER

ANNABEL WINTER STETZ

SHELVIA STEWART

MAIA STRUBLE

EMMA STUBBS

GJ STUCKEY

NAVAH AND MOLLY STUHR

MYA SUMMERFELDT

SYDNEY SUTHERLAND

SIMONE SWINGLE

VICTORIA SZRAMKA

LOLA-IRIS AND LINLEY TA

OLIVIA TAPLEY

HAILEY ADAMS THALMAN

SOPHIE AND VIOLET THI BRANT

LUANA THIBAULT CARRERAS

REBECCA THROPE

PENELOPE TRAYNOR

JULIA TRGOVCEVIC

CAROLINE TUCKER

CORA ELIZABETH TURNER

SONIA TWEITO

ZOOEY TYLER WALKER

AGNES VÅHLUND

FINLEY VARGO

SARAH VASILIDES

SOPHIE VASSER

NOEMI VEIT

RIDHI VEKARIA

GABRIELLA VERBEELEN

NAYARA VIEIRA

FABLE VITALE

GRACE MARIA WAITE

RAEGAN AND DARBY WALSH

TOVA ROSE WASSON

JOSEPHINE WEBSTER-FOX

ELIZABETH WEBSTER-MCFADDEN

ZOE AND TESSA WEINSTEIN

HARPER WEST

LAUREN WEST

STELLA WEST-HUGHES

ANNA WESTENDORF

ELLIA AND VICTORIA WHITACRE

ELEANOR MARIE WHITAKER

MADELYN WHITE

KAYLA WIESEL

GRACE WILLIAMS

TESSANEE AND KIRANNA WILLIAMS

SAM WILSON

VICTORIA PAYTON WOLF

GEMMA WOMACK

TEDDY ROSE WYLDER HEADEY

CHLOE YOUSEFI

HANNAH YUN FEI PHUA

AZUL ZAPATA-TORRENEGRA

SLOANE ZELLER

WILLA AND WINNIE ZIELKE

· ILLUSTRATORS ·

Sixty extraordinary female artists from all over the world portrayed the pioneers in *Good Night Stories for Rebel Girls*. Here are all of them!

T. S. ABE **USA**, 31, 161

CRISTINA AMODEO **ITALY**, 53, 165

ELIZABETH BADDELEY **USA**, 127

ALICE BARBERINI **ITALY**, 139, 191

ELENIA BERETTA **ITALY**, 45

SARA BONDI **ITALY**, 105

MARIJKE BUURLAGE **NETHERLANDS**, 35

CLAUDIA CARIERI **ITALY**, 17, 123, 171

ÉDITH CARRON **FRANCE**, 109

MICHELLE CHRISTENSEN **USA**, 197

JESSICA M. COOPER **USA**, 199

ELEANOR DAVIS **USA**, 169

BARBARA DZIADOSZ **GERMANY**, 93, 159

ZOZIA DZIERŻAWSKA **POLAND**, 75, 87

PAOLA ESCOBAR **COLOMBIA**, 163

GIULIA FLAMINI **ITALY**, 13, 133

ANA GALVAÑ **SPAIN**, 49, 89, 187

MONICA GARWOOD **USA**, 21, 69, 153

DEBORA GUIDI **ITALY**, 111, 141, 175

SAMIDHA GUNJAL **INDIA**, 179

AMANDA HALL **USA**, 121

LEA HEINRICH **GERMANY**, 19, 55

KATHRIN HONESTA **INDONESIA**, 63, 85

ANA JUAN **SPAIN**, 9, 185

ELENI KALORKOTI **SCOTLAND**, 67

BIJOU KARMAN **USA**, 5

PRIYA KURIYAN **INDIA**, 29, 129

JUSTINE LECOUFFE **USA**, 25, 71

KIKI LJUNG **BELGIUM**, 41, 61, 173

MARTA LORENZON **ITALY**, 47

SOPHIA MARTINECK **GERMANY**, 81

SARAH MAZZETTI **ITALY**, 99

KARABO MOLETSANE **SOUTH AFRICA**, 103

HELENA MORAIS SOARES **PORTUGAL**, 59, 149

SALLY NIXON **USA**, 65, 167

MARTINA PAUKOVA **SLOVAKIA**, 125, 137

CAMILLA PERKINS **USA**, 155

RITA PETRUCCIOLI **ITALY**, 79, 147

ZARA PICKEN **USA**, 157

CRISTINA PORTOLANO **ITALY**, 7, 39, 131

KATE PRIOR **USA**, 23, 107

PAOLA ROLLO **ITALY**, 51, 77

MALIN ROSENQVIST **SWEDEN**, 95, 101

DALILA ROVAZZANI **ITALY**, 57

KAROLIN SCHNOOR **GERMANY**, 43

MARTA SIGNORI **ITALY**, 115, 143, 183

NOA SNIR **ISRAEL**, 195, 201

RIIKKA SORMUNEN **FINLAND**, 73

CRISTINA SPANÒ **ITALY**, 113, 117

GAIA STELLA **ITALY**, 119

LIZZY STEWART **UK**, 27

ELISABETTA STOINICH **ITALY**, 3, 33

GERALDINE SY **PHILIPPINES**, 11, 181

THANDIWE TSHABALALA **SOUTH AFRICA**, 135, 189

ELINE VAN DAM **NETHERLANDS**, 15, 177

CARI VANDER YACHT **USA**, 91

LIEKE VAN DER VORST **NETHERLANDS**, 97

EMMANUELLE WALKER **CANADA**, 83

SARAH WILKINS **NEW ZEALAND**, 37, 145

PING ZHU **USA**, 151, 193

· ACKNOWLEDGMENTS ·

Gratitude is one of our favorite feelings. It has accompanied the creation of this book from its inception through the moment you hold it in your hands. Now, as you are about to finish it, we have a few women who are special to us and who we want to thank:

Our mothers, *Lucia* and *Rosa*, who always believed in us and showed us the phenomenal power of a rebel heart, day after day; our newborn niece, *Olivia*, for giving us one more reason to fight the tough fights; *Antonella*, for always being a big sister, despite being the youngest; *Annalisa*, *Brenda*, and *Elettra* who are the most precious friends anyone could ever hope for; *Christine*, who—after a twenty minute meeting—decided that 500startups would become the first investor in Timbuktu Labs; *Arianna*, for her unshaken enthusiasm in all things *Timbuktu* and for her precious collaboration on the research for this book; *Anita*, for being an incredible editor; *Vilma*, for the rock she is; *nonna Marisa*, for her trusting heart and luminous eyes; *nonna Giovanna*, for always keeping it real with the sassiest productivity quotes on earth; *zie Lelle*, for all the laughs.

A heartfelt "thank you" to the (as we're writing) 20,025 backers whose support helped us bring *Good Night Stories for Rebel Girls* to life.

We couldn't have done this without you.

· ABOUT THE AUTHORS ·

ELENA FAVILLI is a media entrepreneur and a journalist. She has worked for *Colors* magazine, McSweeney's, RAI, *Il Post,* and *La Repubblica,* and has managed digital newsrooms on both sides of the Atlantic. She holds a masters degree in semiotics from the University of Bologna (Italy) and she studied digital journalism at U.C. Berkeley. In 2011, she created the first iPad magazine for children, *Timbuktu* magazine. She is the founder and CEO of Timbuktu Labs.

FRANCESCA CAVALLO is a published writer and theater director. Her award-winning plays have been staged all across Europe. A passionate social innovator, Francesca is the founder of Sferracavalli, an International Festival of Sustainable Imagination in Southern Italy. In 2011, Francesca joined forces with Elena Favilli to found Timbuktu Labs, where she serves as Creative Director. *Good Night Stories for Rebel Girls* is her seventh children's book.

Elena and Francesca live in Venice, California.

TIMBUKTU LABS is the children's media innovation lab founded by Elena Favilli and Francesca Cavallo. From books to playgrounds, from mobile games to interactive workshops, Timbuktu is committed to redefining the boundaries of children's media through a combination of thought-provoking content, stellar design, and cutting-edge technology. With 2 million users in more than 70 countries, 12 mobile apps, and 7 books, Timbuktu is building a global community of progressive parents.

Timbuktu's products have won:

- 2016 *Play 60, Play On* (an initiative by the NFL foundation to reinvent public playgrounds)
- 2014 First Special Mention at Bordeaux Biennale of Architecture
- 2013 Best Children's Magazine of the Year at London Digital Magazine Awards
- 2012 Best Design Award at Launch Education and Kids
- 2012 Best Italian Startup

If you want to receive occasional updates about Timbuktu's new projects, subscribe at: www.timbuktu.me

Join the Rebel Girls' community on:
    Facebook: www.facebook.com/timbuktumagazine
    Instagram: @rebelgirlsbook
    Snapchat: @rebelgirlsbook

If you bought this book on Amazon, please take a moment to review it!

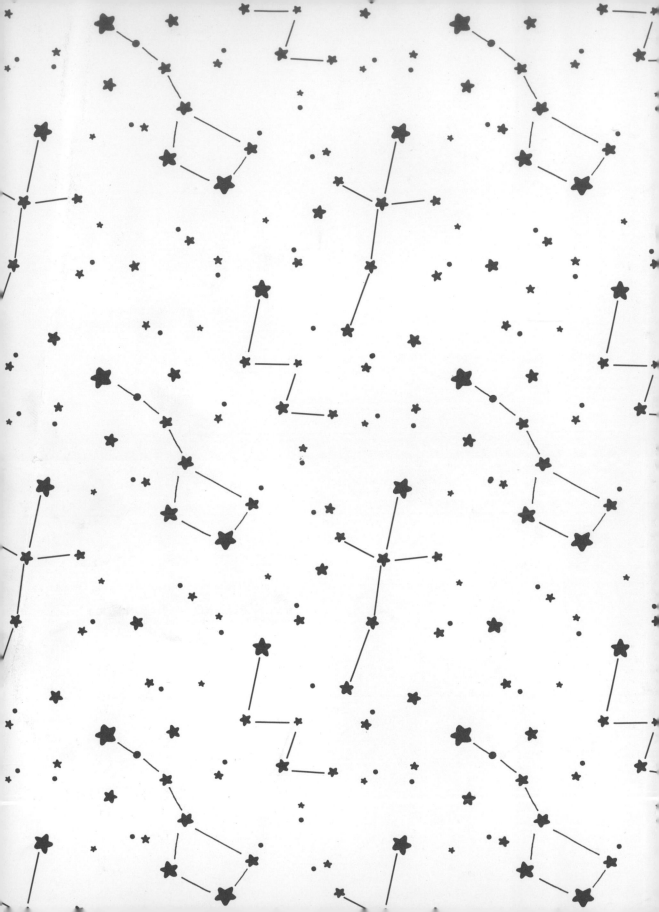